# aCTIHG OUT

*Scenes and Monologues from Theatre Direct Productions for Youth*

# Acting Out:

## Scenes & Monologues from Theatre Direct Productions for Youth

Playwrights Canada Press
Toronto • Canada

**Playwrights Canada Press**
The Canadian Drama Publisher
215 Spadina Avenue, Suite 230, Toronto, Ontario CANADA M5T 2C7
416-703-0013   fax 416-408-3402
orders@playwrightscanada.com • www.playwrightscanada.com

Financial support provided by the taxpayers of Canada and Ontario through the
Canada Council for the Arts and the Department of Canadian Heritage through the
Book Publishing Industry Development Programme, and the Ontario Arts Council.

 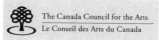 

Production Editor: Michael Petrasek
Front cover: From *Alphonse*, photo by Andrew Oxenham, image manipulation
by lisa kiss design, cover design by JLArt.

**Library and Archives Canada Cataloguing in Publication**

Acting Out : scenes and monologues from Theatre Direct Productions for youth.

Includes index.
ISBN-13: 978-0-88754-882-6
ISBN-10: 0-88754-882-2

1. Monologues, Canadian (English)--21st century. 2. Canadian drama
(English)--21st century. 3. Acting. I. Playwrights Canada Press II. Theatre
Direct Canada

PS8307.A37 2006          C812'.608          C2006-905914-4

First edition: March 2007.
Printed and bound by Canadian Printco at Scarborough, Canada.

The following publishers are acknowledged for giving their permission to include excerpts from the listed works in *Acting Out...*

Fifth House Books, a division of Fitzhenry and Whiteside
*Toronto at Dreamer's Rock*

Scirocco Drama, an imprint of J. Gordon Shillingford Publishing
*Andrew's Tree*
*Boys*
*I Met a Bully on the Hill*
*Misha*
*The Phoenix Rides a Skateboard*

Talonbooks
*Girl Who Loved Her Horses*
*Little Sister*

THEATRE DIRECT CANADA

# Table of Contents

# Introduction

With the publication of this anthology we celebrate our thirty years of Theatre Direct's theatre for young people and offer to drama educators, directors and young actors a dynamic collection of excellent dramatic writing suitable for study and performance in high school, theatre schools and professional training.

This is writing that is demanding and challenges the artist to endow a young character with as much emotional depth and truth as they would an adult character. Whether it is 5-year-old Neil or 12-year-old Patrick, both grieving the loss of their sibling in *Andrew's Tree* or 16-year-old Kim, an Asian adoptee searching for identity in *The Phoenix Rides a Skateboard*; 14-year-old Stacey, pregnant and in denial in *Pop Song* or 12-year-old Anjali, recently arrived in Canada from India in *Beneath the Banyan Tree*; the process of getting inside the heads and hearts of these characters is not only an act of creation and interpretation, it is an act of honouring the complexity of childhood and youth experiences.

As the material is laid out chronologically, *Acting Out* serves as a record of Theatre Direct's dynamic relationship with our audiences and our efforts to keep in touch with the current issues and concerns of young people and to see the world through their eyes. Since the founding of the theatre, the world has changed and young peoples' relationship to the world has changed with it. While the specific issues or subject matter addressed by us have changed to reflect or respond to the times, what has remained constant is are a compelling set of themes at the heart of the plays such as love and friendship, identity, belonging, power, justice and injustice.

The diversity of viewpoints and voices in the plays excerpted for this collection also reflect our refusal to view our audience as a monolith and strive to speak directly to the individual. They are uncompromising and unafraid to expose condradiction and failings in the characters, or to indict the adult world for theirs. Most importantly, these plays share a belief in the power of drama and its potential for provoking young people toward deeper reflection, critical thought, and indeed toward a cathartic theatrical experience. We hope you will be inspired to obtain the full scripts for further reading or production.

A final note. In compiling this collection, we consciously chose not to include works from the very early years of the company, approximately 1976–1985 and plays by founder, and award-winning playwright David Craig, now Artistic Director of Roseneath Theatre. Mr. Craig's extensive body of work demands an entirely distinct consideration, which we hope to see in a future publication.

We hope you enjoy *Acting Out*!

## Acknowledgements

Theatre Direct would like to thank Lisa Codrington and Soraya Peerbaye for their assistance in selecting the scenes.

We are hugely grateful to Elizabeth Helmers for her hard work editing the collection and coordinating the project.

Heartfelt thank yous to Angela Rebeiro who believed in the importance of this project and its value for students, artists and educators.

Thank you to all the playwrights who ageed to have their work included in this collection, and to all the playwrights whose plays make up our 30 years of theatre but could not be included in this publication. We are forever grateful—none of it can happen without your words and vision.

Finally thank you to David Craig for starting it all, and the tremendous leadership of Theatre Direct's Artistic Directors over the years who believed in the importance of commissioning and developing a canon of Canadian theatre for young people.

**Lynda Hill, Artistic Director**

## Foreword

As playwright in residence for Theatre Direct's 2005/2006 season I was given the opportunity to immerse myself in theatre for young audiences. I read plays and unsolicited scripts, attended student performances and workshops and sat in on rehearsals. One of the highlights of my time at Theatre Direct was the opportunity to work on this anthology in tandem with my own research and development for a new piece of my own.

As I began to read some of the plays that Theatre Direct has produced over the years it became clear to me that many of my beliefs about theatre for young audiences were misconceptions. I thought there was a limit as to how honest I was allowed to be, I believed that I would have to compromise my voice somewhat if I was to write for young audiences. So when I began to read the plays, I was amazed at the honest, passionate and engaging stories I encountered.

I was blown away by Kate Rigg's *Phoenix Rides a Skateboard*. A one-woman show that pulls no punches and takes a bold, humorous and poetic look at racism and identity through a multitude of characters. In *Bang Boy Bang!* Edward Roy explores the issue of rape through a multimedia lens and projects an engaging tale about need, power and control. Issues of HIV/AIDS and eating disorders never take precedence over the depth of character in plays like *Flesh and Blood* by Colin Thomas or in *Little Sister* by Joan MacLeod.

Martha Brooks doesn't shy away from heavy subjects in theatre for children. She tackles loss and grieving in *Andrew's Tree* and bullying in *I Met a Bully on the Hill* along with Maureen Hunter. *Not Quite the Same* by Anne Chislett takes a magical look at the ingredients that make up a genius. Drew Hayden Taylor creates heart breaking images one second and then inspiring ones the next in his beautifully written play *Girl Who Loved Her Horses*. *The Demonstration* by Mark Cassidy with the Company is an example of much of the collaborative work that Theatre Direct is engaging in at the moment. Movement, stories, music and debates fuse this kinetic experience together. The students who attended the performances not only got to watch, but participated in the day-long workshops that followed the performances.

These are only a few examples of the fantastic scenes and monologues that you will find in this anthology. Enjoy.

**Lisa Codrington, Playwright-in-Residence, 2004–2005**

## Theatre Direct Productions 1976–2006

| Year | Production | |
|------|------------|---|
| 1976 | *The Clown Who Laughed and Laughed* | Western Tour |
| 1977 | *The Clown Who Laughed and Laughed* | |
| 1978 | *The Great Canadian Energy Show* | |
| | *The Clown Who.../Great Canadian Energy Show* | Western Tour |
| | *The Great Canadian Energy Show* | |
| 1978 | *All for Beaver Hats* | |
| 1979 | *The Great Canadian Energy Show* | Western Tour |
| | *The Great Canadian Energy Show* | |
| | *The Clown Who Laughed and Laughed* | |
| | *All For Beaver Hats* | Ontario/Quebec |
| | *The Great Canadian Energy Show* | |
| | *The Return of the Curious Clown* | |
| 1980 | *The Return of the Curious Clown* | |
| | *All For Beaver Hats* | |
| | *The Great Canadian Energy Show* | |
| | *All For Beaver Hats* | |
| | *The Return of the Curious Clown* | |
| | *Dreamburger Dilemma* | |
| 1981 | *All For Beaver Hats* | Maritimes |
| | *Dreamburger Dilemma* | |
| | *Dreamburger Dilemma* | |
| | *All For Beaver Hats* | Holland/England Germany |
| | *Friendship Fable* | |
| 1982 | + *How I Wonder What You Are* | |
| | *Friendship Fable* | |
| | *How I Wonder What You Are* | |
| 1983 | *The Railroad Story* | |
| | *Morgan's Journey* | |
| | *How I Wonder What You Are* | |
| | *Oscar's Dream* | |
| | *Morgan's Journey* | |
| | *New Canadian Kid* | |
| | *Friends* | |
| | *New Canadian Kid* | |
| | *New Canadian Kid* | |

*Love and Work Enough
1984    Friendship Fable
1985    *Getting Wrecked
        Love and Work Enough
        Getting Wrecked
        *The General
1986    *Double Vision
        How I Wonder What You Are
        *Streetsafe
        The General
        Getting Wrecked
1987    *Peace & Plenty
        + *The Snake Lady
        + *Thin Ice
        The Snake Lady
        The Kingdom of LoudAsCanBe
1988    The General
        Thin Ice
        Thin Ice                        Edmonton Fringe
        Thin Ice                        National Tour
1989    Thin Ice                        Ontario Tour
        *Horror High
        Gil / *Burt (Theatre le Carrousel's production presented by Theatre Direct)
1990    +Andrew's Tree (Originally produced by Prairie Theatre Exchange, PTE)
        Andrew's Tree (Originally produced by PTE)
1991    I Met a Bully on the Hill (Originally produced by PTE)
        + *Flesh and Blood (Originally commissioned by Green Thumb
        Theatre For Young People)
        Toronto At Dreamer's Rock (Originally produced by
        De-ba-jeh-mu-jig Theatre)
1992    I Met A Bully On The Hill
        Flesh and Blood
        Toronto at Dreamer's Rock          Touring Ontario
1993    Toronto at Dreamer's Rock          Vancouver /
                                           Calgary / Winnipeg
        + *A Secret Life
        Andrew's Tree
1994    + *Little Sister
        ++ Hippopotamus Tea
        A Secret Life

**1995**  *Girl Who Loved Her Horses*
*Toronto at Dreamer's Rock*
**1996**  + *Napalm the Magnificent*
*Little Sister*
*U.F.O.R.E.X.*
**1997**  *Little Sister*
*End of Season* (Canadian premiere – Premiere at Red Ladder, UK)
**1998**  + *The General*
*Bang Boy Bang!* (Ontario premiere TDC – Premiere at Youtheatre, Montreal)
*Bang Boy Bang!*
**1999**  ++ *Waiting For Lewis*
*The General*
**2000**  Buncha young artists havin' their say... Festival:
* 1. *Boys*
* 2. *Vicious Little Boyz in the Rain*
   3. *Pop Song*
* 4. *Karma*

*Not Quite the Same*
*Not Quite the Same*
**2001**  *Trickster Tale*
**2002**  *Andrew's Tree*
Buncha Young Artists Festival:
1. *Martian Summer*
2. *Roundabout*
3. *Misha*
4. *The Phoenix Rides a Skateboard*

*Alphonse* (English-language premiere, new translation)
**2003**  *I Met a Bully On the Hill*
*Petra* (Canadian premiere – Premiere at Tag Theatre Scotland)
*Petra*
**2004**  *Andrew's Tree*
*And by the way, Miss...*
**2005**  *Andrew's Tree*
*Beneath the Banyan Tree* (Premiered by Sampradaya Dance Creations in association with Theatre Direct)
**2006**  *Beneath the Banyan Tree*
*The Demonstration*

* Denotes Premiere
+ Denotes Chalmers Award
++ Denotes Chalmers Nomination

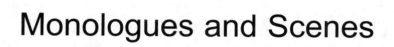

Monologues and Scenes

## *The General* by Robert Morgan

ROBERT MORGAN is the founding Artistic Director of the Children's Peace Theatre and the founding artistic co-director of Roseneath Theatre, both based in Toronto, Canada. He has written more than twenty plays and has acted in and directed more than forty productions. He has won the Chalmers Award for outstanding playwrighting six times, and four of his plays have won Toronto's Dora Mavor Moore Award for best production. His work has received a total of ten Dora nominations and has been performed around the world.

ဢ    ဢ    ဢ

### Synopsis

Frank Groff was known to his community as "The Bridgeport General." Every day for seventeen years, the 63-year-old Bridgeport resident had volunteered his services as the local school's crossing guard. In 1973 he was dismissed from his post after the regional government annexed the small village to the City of Kitchener. Led by their children, the local residents staged an immediate demonstration demanding the reinstatement of the General. Robert Morgan's stage adaptation of *The General*, based on Frank Etherington's book of the same name, dramatized the events that led to his dismissal and eventually turned the General into a local hero.

This story is retold through the experiences of 7-year-old JAININ and her 8-year-old brother, JACOB.

The full script of *The General* is available through Playwrights Guild of Canada, www.playwrightsguild.ca.

## The General

*JAININ bursts into the house startling JACOB.*

**JAININ**  Jacob we have to stop them!

**JACOB**  Jainin you're going to give me a heart attack.

**JAININ**  Whose crossing guard is he anyway? Whose?! Whose?!

**JACOB**  Jainin...?

**JAININ**  Us kids, that's who!

**JACOB**  Jainin you're losing it.

**JAININ**  If they want to fire him they have to ask us first.

**JACOB**  Okay you're right. But fire who?

**JAININ**  The General!

**JACOB**  The General?!

**JAININ**  The General. They want to fire the General, Jacob, and nobody asked us!

**JACOB**  They can't do that.

**JAININ**  You're darn right they can't. He's been at that crossing for ever, before Kitchener even thought about having crossing guards.

**JACOB**  They can't come in here and take over our village.

**JAININ**  I'm not going to sit around and let them do that to my friend.

**JACOB**  None of us kids will.

**JAININ**  We've got rights and we're going to do something.

**JACOB**  You're darn right we are! What?

**JAININ**  Well, we'll start with a list of all the people who want the General to stay.

**JACOB**  Great idea! We'll write a petition. And take it around for the whole village to sign.

**JAININ**   And we'll start right now.

**JACOB**   Yah. They can't just get rid of people like that.

**JAININ**   (writing) "To the Kitchener City Council and the person in charge of crossing-guards." Okay, what should I say?

**JACOB**   Tell 'em we don't want the Bridgeport General fired from his job as school-crossing guard.

**JAININ**   Good. That's good.

**JACOB**   Tell 'em we want 'em to give him back his job. Now!

**JAININ**   Good. That's really good.

**JACOB**   Tell 'em this stunt they're trying to pull isn't fair and we want it stopped. Now!

**JAININ**   Yes.

**JACOB**   I'll make copies of the petition and deliver them to the Sunoco station, the hotel, the post office and the village clerk...

**JAININ**   And we'll take some to school.

**JACOB**   Wait a minute!

**JAININ**   What?

**JACOB**   You're not going to believe this!

**JAININ**   What?

**JACOB**   I've got a great idea.

**JAININ**   You're right. I don't believe it.

**JACOB**   No. I'm incredible. I learned about it last week in social studies. It's about how to change things. You know when Dad was weird with the long hair and flowers, well back then there was a war and there were a bunch of people who wanted to stop the war and they wanted everybody to know that it should be stopped. So you know what they did?

**JAININ**   What did they do?

**JACOB**   They used the television. They infiltrated the existing media to publicate their cause. They got themselves on TV, it didn't cost them a cent and it worked. They stopped the war. Now we can do the same thing. Jainin! We should phone the TV station.

**JAININ**  Yeah, and Garth's mom works for the newspaper. She could tell them.

**JACOB**  Yeah, but we've got to do something that'll make the newspaper and TV news people take notice.

**JAININ**  We should do what they do on the news all the time.

**JACOB**  Take hostages?

**JAININ**  No. We should make big signs and march around at the General's crossing.

**JACOB**  That's a protest!

**JAININ**  Yeah! We should do a protest.

**JACOB**  Jainin you're brilliant. A non-violent protest. Just like our teachers did! We'll have a demonstration. We're talking social justice, decency, and doing the right thing!

**JAININ**  We'll show 'em they can't mess with our General.

## *Thin Ice* by Bañuta Rubess & Beverley Cooper

BAÑUTA RUBESS is a director and writer with a string of innovative productions to her credit. A Rhodes Scholar with a doctorate in history, Rubess has been living with her family in Riga, Latvia. She returns to Canada now and then, notably to direct new opera. Her most recent achievements are *Fruits of the Earth*, a piece about cooking and childbirth for saxophones and choir; *Escape from Troy*, a performance for actors, choir and marching band; and the chamber opera *Oh Pilot*.

BEVERLEY COOPER has written for theatre, television and film. She has also written extensively for CBC radio drama; from the 1992 *Psychic Driving*, a searing look at the CIA brainwashing experiments in Montréal; to the popular series, *The Super Adventures of Mary Marvelous*. Beverley has also dramatized many novels for radio, including Rohinton Mistry's *A Fine Balance*; for which Beverley was nominated for a Writer's Guild of Canada Award. She is also an actor, performing in television, film and theatre.

෴ ෴ ෴

**Synopsis**

*Thin Ice* is a play for adolescents that deals with the issue of sexual coercion, examining the subtle and not-so-subtle forces that encourage sexually coercive relationships.

At the beginning of the play, we learn that TONY's parents are going away for the weekend and that he is having a party. During two parallel sequences, gossip focuses on the rumours about TONY's older brother, Ron, who is alleged to have raped a girl while he was out on a date with her. JENNIFER and TRISH find it difficult to believe the rumours as Ron is a very attractive and popular guy who certainly does not fit the usual stereotypes of the "typical rapist."

Early in the play, a relationship develops between TONY and JENNIFER and he invites her to the party as his special guest. To make certain that JENNIFER will "show up," TONY talks DES into inviting her best friend, TRISH. The party turns out to be a valuable experience for everyone.

The full script of *Thin Ice* is available through Playwrights Guild of Canada, www.playwrightsguild.ca.

## *Thin Ice*

**JENNIFER**   Do you think I can wear what I'm wearing?

**TRISH**   Are you crazy? It's got to be really sexy.

**JENNIFER**   No!!!

**TRISH**   Oh, Mother Theresa. You want to see him again, don't you?

**JENNIFER**   What if he kisses me and... you know, he goes for it.

**TRISH**   Do you want to?

**JENNIFER**   I don't know.

**TRISH**   You had better decide before you go.

**JENNIFER**   What if he, you know, kisses me and then slips me the tongue? *(makes a face)*

**TRISH**   Oh, c'mon, you've kissed before.

**JENNIFER**   Stuart doesn't count. And that time at Donna's party was kind of sick.

**TRISH**   Listen, you get used to it, I promise... I'm going to lend you that red dress of mine.

**JENNIFER**   Uh uh, I'll look like a whore.

**TRISH**   That's the point, bimbo brain. You don't think he asked you out for intellectual stimulation, do you?

**JENNIFER**   Don't you hate it when you find yourself in a situation... with a guy... that you don't know how to get out of.

**TRISH**   Like what?

**JENNIFER**   Well like... what if Des takes you out to a movie and then for something to eat and then he expects something in return. Just because he paid for everything.

**TRISH**   I don't have to give it to him. If I don't want to. *(laughs)*

**JENNIFER**   Did you hear what happened to BJ? So she didn't want to do it, not at least until they knew each other for eight months or something, and then her boyfriend caught her talking to another guy and said now or else.

And she didn't really want to. And now they've broken up and he's calling her a slut. He's the slut, if you ask me.

**TRISH**   Just remember: Every girl in school would pay to be in your situation, don't let us all down. You can have your meaningful relationship next year. Anyway, it's gotta happen sometime, if you sit around and wait, the only people left will be the dregs of society.

**JENNIFER**   Tony's really cute.

**TRISH**   So what are you waiting for, Harry from your computer class? Give me a break.

## *Thin Ice*

*DES and TRISH parked in front of TRISH's place. TRISH*
*wants DES to kiss her and more... she expects him to. But he*
*won't make a move.*

**TRISH**   Well thanks for driving me home. And thanks for the
dinner and everything... I don't think I've ever been anywhere so elegant.

**DES**   Yeah my uncle took me there once.

*Pause.*

**TRISH**   So...

**DES**   I really like talking to you. Especially what you said about
being an individualist and everything. I think it was Voltaire
who said people should change society as they see fit.

**TRISH**   Yeah...

*Pause.*

**DES**   So what do you think about this terrorist thing?

**TRISH**   Let's not talk about that. *(She undoes her hair.)* Funny,
I don't feel like getting out of the car. It's so comfortable here.
Nobody's at home anyway. Well, except my kid sister but she
keeps to her room.

*Pause.*

**DES**   Well, see you in class on Monday...

**TRISH**   Aren't you going to kiss me goodnight or anything?

**DES**   Oh, sure. *(He pecks her on the cheek.)*

*TRISH stays there with her eyes closed. Nothing happens.*

So. Goodnight.

**TRISH**   Yeah, well, call me sometime.

*The following two monologues are simultaneous.*

Oh my God I can't believe what just happened. Do I have
rabies or what?? Maybe he's got some disease and he doesn't

want to give it to me... or more likely he thought I was stupid and boring and ugly...

I thought guys wanted to have sex. Well maybe they want it only when you don't want to dish it out... maybe he's lurking outside in the bushes and he's going to wait until I'm not suspecting *(very dramatic)* and then he's going to rush in and... talk about terrorism *(pause)* ...or maybe I should call him... (Maybe he really likes me.)

**DES**    SHIT...

Why did I just do that?

She asks me to kiss her and I peck her on the cheek...

She was asking for it... I should have gone for it.

>    *Pause.*

What do they expect? If you grab them they think you're a weirdo and if you don't they think you're a weirdo... you can't win. I just didn't feel like it... I like her. I like talking to her... I don't want to mess that up. Shit.... She asked me to kiss her... maybe I should call her. (Maybe she really likes me.)

## *Thin Ice*

*TONY's place. TONY and JENNIFER. The music of some up-
to-date female singer is playing—e.g. Madonna, Pretenders,
Annie Lennox.*

**JENNIFER**    I saw her you know.

**TONY**    She's something else. Anyone ever tell you you look like
her?

**JENNIFER**    I love the way she dances... I guess the dishes can
wait a little.

**TONY**    Too bad you'd already seen the movie. There's only one
thing left to do now.

*They kiss. Disengage with some embarrassment.*

**JENNIFER**    What?

*(aside)* He's looking so intense. I think he really likes me.

**TONY**    *(aside)* I wonder how that bra works?

**JENNIFER**    *(aside)* Wait till I tell Trish... she'll just die.

**TONY**    *(aside)* She's no virgin. Look at that dress. If I just move
my hand around the side, maybe she won't notice.

**JENNIFER**    *(aside)* Wait a minute—does he think I don't know
what he's doing? *(to him)* Hey, Tony—

**TONY**    Did anyone ever tell you you have the most beautiful
eyes in the world? *(aside)* I spent twenty bucks on beer
tonight.

**JENNIFER**    No. *(aside)* He wasn't looking in my eyes.

**TONY**    *(embracing her)* C'mon. Let's get to know each other.
*(aside)* Nice n' easy.

*They kiss again.*

**JENNIFER**    You've got nice eyes too. *(aside)* I think I just broke
a rib.

**TONY**    You make me feel... *(aside)* What a tease... she's not
going to stop now.

**JENNIFER**   When are your parents coming home? *(aside)* He's got to know I don't want to... maybe if I cross my legs...

**TONY**   They're gonna be gone for ages... *(aside)* She must be really hot, she just crossed her legs...

**JENNIFER**   I'm really tired. *(aside)* There, I said it. What if he doesn't ask me out again?

**TONY**   You don't mean that. *(aside)* Relax for crissake!!!

*He pours a beer and makes her drink it.*

Bottoms up!!!

**JENNIFER**   Tony!

*TONY kisses her. He puts his hand on her knee, starts pulling up her skirt.*

**JENNIFER**   Please...

**TONY**   This is getting monotonous. What's wrong with you? You a virgin or something?

**JENNIFER**   I hardly even know you.

**TONY**   C'mon, Jennifer, everybody does it.

**JENNIFER**   So if everyone jumped off the CN Tower would you?

**TONY**   Oh, I get it, you're frigid.

**JENNIFER**   No.

**TONY**   You're just trying to protect your precious reputation. *(He grabs her arm and pushes her down on the couch.)* C'mon, I know you want it.

**JENNIFER**   Look, it's late, I'm tired.

**TONY**   You've turned me on, now you've got to.

**JENNIFER**   I can't believe this is happening.

**TONY**   If you don't help me I'll rip it off.

*JENNIFER struggles with him. He starts to take a swipe at her. They freeze.*

**TONY**   *(aside)* I can't believe I almost hit her. It's OK. I didn't do anything wrong. C'mon crybaby. Just relax.

**JENNIFER**  (*aside*) I should have said no. Why didn't I just say NO. It's all my fault. I feel sick.

> *Break from the freeze. JENNIFER jumps up and turns up the music very loud.*

**TONY**  Hey it's two o'clock in the morning. The neighbours are gonna—

> *JENNIFER grabs her coat and shoes. The phone rings and there is a knocking at the door. TONY answers the phone.*

No, Mrs. Chong. Yes, I'll turn it right down.

> *He goes to the door, we hear someone haranguing him.*

I'm sorry sir, it won't happen again.

> *TONY turns down the volume. JENNIFER and TONY look at each other. TONY steps towards her. JENNIFER jumps back.*

**JENNIFER**  Keep away from me.

**TONY**  Look, I'm sorry. OK? I'll drive you home.

**JENNIFER**  Don't come any closer.

**TONY**  I promise not to touch you, OK? What are ya, a prude?

**JENNIFER**  You're just an animal. You're not even human. You're sick. You're a rapist.

**TONY**  Give me a break! Just because I tried to cop a feel?

**JENNIFER**  You weren't going to stop.

**TONY**  So?

**JENNIFER**  So you just can't wait to tell the guys you scored. You and your precious little ego.

**TONY**  Look, you knew what was going on.

**JENNIFER**  So did you.

> *Pause.*

**TONY**  Let me drive you home.

**JENNIFER**  (*picks up the phone and dials*) Hi, I'd like a cab to 360 Maplethorpe...

> *TONY and JENNIFER freeze.*

## *Horror High* by Bañuta Rubess

*See Bañuta Rubess' biography on page 8.*

ဢ ဢ ဢ

### Synopsis

SPHINX (a.k.a. Martina) and LEIF (a.k.a. Eric) are two morbid sixteen-year-olds who meet during a horror movie at a revue cinema. On their way home with the grumpy projectionist, SAM, they get carried away playing chicken on the subway platform. They pull SAM into the game; he falls and dies. With the shock of SAM's death, their story begins.

SPHINX escapes from the difficulties of her life into rich fantasies of death and the occult. She is convinced that SAM committed suicide and that he must be exorcised. LEIF, on the other hand, is in the throes of adolescent pressures. He begins to perceive the real world as peopled by monsters. Once he considers SAM as a suicide, he contemplates following SAM's example. He tries to communicate his distress and intentions to SPHINX, but she cannot read the signals and does not take his cries for help seriously until it is almost too late.

The full script of *Horror High* is available through Theatre Direct.

## *Horror High*

*SPHINX and LEIF are at SAM'S funeral at an outside*
*cemetery. SPHINX is holding a wreath.*

**SPHINX**      *(rising hysteria)* I told him to do it, I said jump! I said
jump! *(calming)* Now stop that. It was a stupid accident a stupid accident that's all. He lost his balance.
*(rising hysteria)* I made him do it. I made him fall.
I shouted at him and he lost his concentration.
This is really bad karma.
*(calming)* Now stop that Martina! Are you a Sphinx or what?
Stiff upper lip like the Gram always says! It was an accident.
An accident is an accident. No blame.

He was the funniest guy. Always some crazy idea.

The time we all wore gorilla masks. The night he was the
phantom of the cinema and the boss walked in.

I bet that's his mother over there. She must be really cut up.
Where's Leif? Hiding in the back row. What a stupid name.
I wonder if *he* cried at the police station.

Will you stop your preachy droning. Ashes to ashes bla bla
bla. Dontcha know we had a living person over here. He had
more life in the tip of his noseknob than you've got in your
whole ugly body. He held my hand all through "Nightmare
on Elm Street Part Three." Like he hardly knew me, OK, but
he held it anyway.

He was my only friend here. And now he's gone.

This just can't be happening. Any minute now Sam will jump
out from the bushes and say "boo!" Please?

## *Andrew's Tree* by Martha Brooks

MARTHA BROOKS received the Governor General's Award for her young adult novel, *True Confessions of a Heartless Girl*. She is, as well, recipient of the Mr. Christie's Book Award, the Vicky Metcalf Award, the *Boston Globe*/Horn Book Honor Award, and the Canadian Library Association's Young Adult Book Award for her titles, *Being With Henry, Paradise Cafe and Other Stories*, and *Bone Dance*. Martha is also a jazz singer. Her CD "Change of Heart," won the 2002 Prairie Music Award for Outstanding Jazz Recording.

ꜱ ꜱ ꜱ

**Synopsis**

Four months ago PATRICK DEVEREAUX's five-year-old brother, Andrew, was struck down and killed by a car. PATRICK is caught in an endless merry-go-round of guilt and denial. He has withdrawn from both family and friends, unable to express his grief.

Then the Peterson family moves in next door. The three children deal with losing their friends each time they move. This move is the second for NEIL, a lonely five-year-old, whose friends include imaginary buffaloes and his best friend, a lively baby rabbit named Sparky. SARAH is a nine-year-old ballet student who is caught in the unenviable position of middle child. GILLIAN is twelve and has left behind her best friend after her fourth move. Despite their own losses, and PATRICK's hostility, they try to befriend their new neighbour.

The full script of *Andrew's Tree* is available through Scirocco Drama, an imprint of J. Gordon Shillingford Publishing, www.jgshillingford.com.

## Andrew's Tree

*PATRICK is drawing stick figures of his family on the fence. NEIL enters and approaches PATRICK.*

**NEIL** I'm Neil Alexander Peterson. I got a buffalo ranch. Know how many buffaloes I have to feed every day? *(He waits for a response, doesn't get it, plunges ahead.)* Two hundred. That's a lot of buffaloes. And I had to bring them all with me from our old house. In our car. It took three days and two sleets to get here—sheesh! *(beat)* Do you have a brother I could play with?

**PATRICK** He's... gone away.

*PATRICK wipes away the "Andrew" stick figure.*

**NEIL** Did he go to camp? Gillian hated camp. They made her eat terrible food. That smelled.

*PATRICK ignores him and continues to scrape the fence.*

*(cheerfully)* Before I had my rabbit, Sparky, I had two goldfish. One was named Sunny and the other was Finny. They died. Mom flushed them down the toilet. I wouldn't go to the bathroom for two whole days.

**PATRICK** Good for you.

**NEIL** I was scared they'd come up and bite my bum. *(beat)* Is it fun to do that?

**PATRICK** It's a million laughs.

**NEIL** Gillian's twelve. She's getting paid three-fifty an hour to look after Sarah and me. How much is your dad paying you?

**PATRICK** He's not paying me. It's something to do.

**NEIL** Gillian never lets me help. She's saving up for a Black 'n' Decker table saw.

**PATRICK** Gee. Hope she doesn't cut herself.

**NEIL** Do you have another one of those?

**PATRICK** *(turning on him)* Look. I only have one lonely scraper. And one lonely fence. And I want to do my work—alone.

**NEIL**     When's your brother coming back?

**PATRICK**     When are you going to get lost?

**NEIL**     I have a friend, Robbie. At my other house that's far away? He's five years old. How old's your brother?

**PATRICK**     FIVE! Can't you see I don't want to talk to you? Can't you leave me alone?

*PATRICK advances on NEIL.*

**NEIL**     *(backing away)* What's his name?

**PATRICK**     Andrew!

**NEIL**     *(in a rush)* When Andrew gets back could you tell him that Neil wants to play with him?

*SARAH and GILLIAN enter. A pencil is propped behind GILLIAN's ear and wood shavings are caught in her hair. NEIL runs to meet them. PATRICK grabs a piece of sandpaper and vehemently rubs a section of paint that the scraper has missed.*

*(rejoicing)* Guess what! He has a brother.

**SARAH**     Good for him. *(pleasantly calling out to PATRICK)* We're back—and we're going to kill you!

**GILLIAN**     *(sotto voce)* Shut up, Sarah. We can't negotiate if we start a war. I'll do the talking.

**NEIL**     *(loudly)* What does negotiate mean?

**SARAH**     *(pouting)* It means Gillian will do all the talking as usual, when we tell our weirdo neighbour that Sparky's hutch is going over there. *(raising her voice)* In our bushes!

**NEIL**     But Sparky doesn't want a rabbit house. He wants to stay with me.

**GILLIAN**     You cannot play with a rabbit and imaginary buffaloes for the rest of your life. You have to find real friends, Neil.

**NEIL**     Patrick's brother, Andrew? He's five years old.

**SARAH**     Good. Go and play with him.

**NEIL**     *(disgusted)* Can't. He's at camp.

**GILLIAN**    At camp? He's only five years old.

**SARAH**    Shows how much you know. Sometimes five-year-olds go to day-camp.

> *The Peterson children move en masse toward PATRICK's fence.*

**NEIL**    Why does Sparky have to have a house?

**SARAH**    Use the correct term. They're called hutches.

**GILLIAN**    It'll be much healthier for him to be outside in his own little place. In the fresh air.

**NEIL**    Sparky hates fresh air.

**SARAH**    It's disgusting the way you carry him around all the time. In your shirt. The air in there'll kill him.

**GILLIAN**    *(stopping)* Don't tell him that. You'll scare him.

> *NEIL and SARAH stop, too.*

**SARAH**    *(indignantly)* That rabbit poos and pees in there. It is so gross!

> *As the family argument escalates, so does PATRICK's frustration at being pulled out of himself.*

**NEIL**    Does not!

**SARAH**    What do you call last night when Mom went to give you a bath? Little brown nuggets all over the floor.

**PATRICK**    Go and argue someplace else.

**NEIL**    He'll hate that hutch. He'll be lonely. He won't have any friends.

**GILLIAN**    I have spent two whole days making that dumb rabbit a home. I did it for you, Neil Alexander Peterson, and you'd better be grateful.

**NEIL**    But I didn't...

**PATRICK**    *(blasting them)* I'd be grateful if you'd all drop dead!

**NEIL**    *(in a vehement whisper)* I didn't want it in the first place.

**SARAH**    Shush!

*GILLIAN approaches PATRICK, with SARAH and NEIL close behind.*

**GILLIAN**    *(Emily Post—coolly polite)* We need to talk to you.

**PATRICK**    Too bad. I'm busy.

**SARAH**    *(whispering to GILLIAN)* He is the rudest boy.

**NEIL**    His name is Patrick Devereaux.

**GILLIAN**    I'm Gillian. Peterson. We are the Peterson family. This is my sister, Sarah, and this is…

**PATRICK**    I know who you all are. Stay in your yard! I'll stay in mine. We'll get along swell.

**SARAH**    Well! I can certainly see why you're always alone. If you want to be friends with us, you're going to have to stop being so… pestilent!

**NEIL &
GILLIAN**    Pestilent?

**PATRICK**    You people are unbelievable. I'm not interested in arguing with you. I don't want to be friends! Read my lips— I. Want. To. Be. Left. Alone!

**NEIL**    Why?

*PATRICK is ready to explode, then thinks again. Menacingly, he comes at NEIL.*

**PATRICK**    Because I'm actually a bad, bad wizard. I can make you disappear. I kill little boys with a single thought—that's how powerful I am. I do bloody, diabolical deeds right here. This is my dungeon.

*Stunned silence.*

**NEIL**    *(aghast and fascinated)* Let's see you do one.

## Andrew's Tree

**PATRICK**    I get bad dreams all the time. Every night it's the same dream. I'm standing in front of Andrew's tree—just looking. All of a sudden it becomes a merry-go-round, with painted horses dancing a slow circle. Their smiling mouths are red as apples, and I choose one—a sky blue stallion. *(jumps into the circle)* It takes me into its circle. I'm looking for Andrew. I search all the faces in the crowd. I know he's out there… somewhere. If I could only get my horse to break loose. To break free. But all it knows is the circle. So I have to keep going around and around. Waiting. Hoping. And just when I think I'll never see him—there! Out in the crowd. His blue hat. Andrew—over here! *(waves)* Wait for me, okay? Don't go away this time. *(twists his head as he circles past)* I said, *wait!* *(The music slows. PATRICK jumps out of the circle.)* Come back… Andrew? *(music fades)* Then, I'm awake. I stare up into the dark in my room. And I hear the wind rattling the trees outside my window. And then I remember all over again. My brother wasn't really there. It was just another dream. And I go back to sleep. *(beat)* I wonder what it's like— to sleep and never wake up.

> *PATRICK returns to his work. NEIL enters, dressed as "Buffalo Pete." Over his summer shirt, he wears a black vest with a sheriff's badge. SPARKY is tucked inside his shirt. On his feet are black gum-rubber boots. He wears shorts and a white straw cowboy hat with a chin strap. It is much too big for him. He rummages around under the porch steps and comes out with a bed-roll (an old blanket clumsily held together with twine, which he slings over his shoulder) and a white hobby-horse.*

**NEIL**    *(swinging his leg over "Sheila")* Gidday-up, girl! *(He begins a wide circle of the merry-go-round tree.)* Buffalo Pete and his horse, Sheila, are riding to the ranch. Riding, riding, riding. Gotta feed those buffaloes, Sheila. Look! There's Sherman— my biggest and best buffalo.

> *NEIL drops his bed-roll and Sheila. He swaggers over to an enormous imaginary buffalo.*

Boy! You sure are some big buffalo, Sherman. Big as a house. Big as a Mountain. Big as the whole world!

*PATRICK begins to smile.*

*(pulling air out of his pocket)* Like some Smarties? *(holding out his hand)* I saved all the purple and green ones for you 'cause they're my favourites and Sparky doesn't like them—Hey! Don't eat my hand—oh brother! *(pats the bulge in his shirt)* How're you doing, Sparky. Want to camp out here, tonight? *(He pulls aside the neck of his shirt and puts his ear down, listening.)*

PATRICK    Still got that rabbit inside your shirt?

NEIL    *(startled)* Hi, wizard. *(nervously)* I'm not standing on your property.

PATRICK    My little brother had a hat just like yours.

NEIL    *(encouraged)* I'm Buffalo Pete. And that's my horse, Sheila.

PATRICK    His hat wasn't white. It was blue—so bright it hurt your eyes just looking at it.

NEIL    I wanted a blue horse, but Gillian painted her white because she said there's no such thing as blue horses.

PATRICK    Horses can be any colour you want.

NEIL    It's too late now, Sheila's dead white.

PATRICK    Just close your eyes. Anything can happen.

NEIL    *(closing his eyes)* Like this?

PATRICK    Sometimes in dreams I see my brother.

NEIL    I see Sheila.

PATRICK    What colour is she?

NEIL    *(with delight)* She's blue! *(opens his eyes)* Same colour as your scarf. *(slightly spooked)* How did you do that?

PATRICK    *(adjusting his scarf)* Told you. I'm a wizard. I have magical powers.

NEIL    Is your scarf magic?

**PATRICK**    (*mysteriously*) Maybe.

>    *Pause.*

**NEIL**    Nah! I did it myself. I pretend all the time.

**PATRICK**    The scarf *is* magic.

>    *Beat.*

**NEIL**    (*wondrously believing*) It is? What does it do?

**PATRICK**    It keeps away evil spirits. If you wear it you never have to die.

**NEIL**    I'm never going to die. (*beat*) Do wizards die?

**PATRICK**    Never.

**NEIL**    I won't die for a very very long long long long long long time. Because I'm five. Want to see my rabbit?

**PATRICK**    (*amused, indulging him*) Do I have to close my eyes?

**NEIL**    You're crazy! Sparky's real. He's my best friend. (*pulls neck of his shirt far out*)

**PATRICK**    (*peering inside*) He's very small. (*pulls gently away*)

**NEIL**    That's because he's a baby.

**PATRICK**    What's wrong with his ears?

**NEIL**    He's a lop rabbit, coo-coo brain. Their ears don't stick up. They stick down.

**PATRICK**    He's very young. You'll have to take good care of him.

**NEIL**    When your brother Andrew gets back from camp, I'll let him put Sparky in his shirt if he likes. But you'd better tell him, first, Sparky poos and pees. A lot. (*PATRICK quickly goes back to the fence and begins to paint.*) You could hold him, if you like. Want to be friends with him? Then we could all be friends and when Andrew gets back we could be... (*counting his fingers*) Four friends...

**PATRICK**    He's not coming back!

>    *Pause.*

**NEIL**    (*stricken*) They're making him stay at camp? Forever?

## Toronto at Dreamer's Rock
## by Drew Hayden Taylor

DREW HAYDEN TAYLOR is an Ojibway from the Curve Lake First Nations. A writer of many disciplines, he has produced work for television, movies, and theatre, and has written short stories, commentaries, essays, and whatever else he can get paid for. He has also taught workshops in scriptwriting/playwriting for Native people and visible minorities. Drew was nominated for the Governor General's Literary Award for Drama in 2006 for his play *In A World Created by a Drunken God*.

ဢ ဢ ဢ

### Synopsis

RUSTY, a modern Odawa teenager, has made the long climb to the top of Dreamer's Rock. For thousands of years, Dreamer's Rock has been the sacred site of vision quests for his people. RUSTY, however, is equipped with a walkman and a knapsack from which the clink of bottles can be heard. A crow tries to 'speak' to him but he ignores it and finds himself doing a traditional crow hop dance against his will. As the dance concludes, RUSTY collapses and is magically met by KEESIC, a youth of similar age but from a time several hundred years before. Soon, they are startled by the appearance of another youth, MICHAEL. He is also from another era, this time about one hundred years in the future. The three lads grapple with questions about why they have been brought together to have this "toronto" at Dreamer's Rock.

The full script of *Toronto at Dreamer's Rock* is available from Fifth House, an imprint of Fitzhenry and Whiteside, www.fitzhenry.ca.

## *Toronto at Dreamer's Rock*

**RUSTY**    Do I got a choice? Does it really matter? Okay, I can't go to Hawaii. I'll never own a Porsche, I'll never have all those things I see on the television. I'm lucky if I get a new pair of jeans for the first day of school. What's there to be happy for? I'm terrible in school so I can't walk that side of the tracks, as for going the traditional Indian route, that's even worse. I hate cleaning fish and I'm a terrible hunter. Last year my father took me hunting, I shot my own dog. I don't fit in here. I can't do anything right except drink. You wanted to know my problems, there they are. I hope you enjoy them.

*Everybody is silent for a moment, letting the emotion sink in.*

**MICHAEL**    Ah poor Rusty. Everybody has problems, but they cope with them.

**RUSTY**    Oh yeah? Look at you. I have no idea what kind of outfit that is but it don't look like you're too bad off. And judging by the way you talk and the things you've said, you're doing great in school and you know a lot of things. Keesic here only has to worry about hunting enough to eat. They didn't have complicated problems back then. At least you both have your own worlds to fit in and return to. I'm stuck smack dab in the middle of a family war, between one uncle that's called "Closer" because they say he's closed every bar in Ontario, and my other Uncle Stan, who is basically a Pow Wow Indian, I never know what's going on. I don't know if I should go into a Sweatlodge or a liquor store. Sometimes they tear me apart. I don't fit in. Like tonight. It's Saturday and what am I doing? Standing on a rock out in the middle of the woods talking to two people who probably don't exist. How's that for a social life? Instead of looking at the two of you, I should be out with some hot babe. *(to himself)* I should have asked her out. I should have.

## *Flesh and Blood* by Colin Thomas

COLIN THOMAS works as a playwright and theatre critic. The Chalmers Children's Playwriting Awards have honoured each of his three most recent works for young audiences—*One Thousand Cranes*; *Two Weeks, Twice a Year*; and *Flesh and Blood*. Companies across Canada and throughout the United States continue to mount these scripts. Prestigious American productions include those at The Mark Taper Forum in Los Angeles and The Kennedy Centre in Washington, DC. *Sex is My Religion*, Thomas's first play for adult theatregoers, has been produced in Vancouver, Toronto, Ottawa, Houston, and New York. John Alleyne, artistic director of Ballet B.C., has created a dance version. Thomas has been the theatre critic for *The Georgia Straight* for 20 years.

ഗ ഗ ഗ

### Synopsis

JIM has been diagnosed as having AIDS. He must confront the overwhelming realities of his disease and how his condition will also affect his younger and rebellious brother, ALLAN, a reluctant high school student. ALLAN has always depended on JIM to be brother, friend and even a father-figure in a family strained by their parents' incompatibility. But now JIM must make the biggest decision of his life. Will he allow ALLAN, and his love RALPH, to care for him as his condition deteriorates? Can a teenager like ALLAN even handle such responsibilities? Would it be better to deny the existence of AIDS to himself and live with the shadowy consequences of the future?

The full script of *Flesh and Blood* is available from Theatre Direct.

## *Flesh and Blood*

**SHERRI**     Al-Guy. I don't know where you are right now, but I want you to get this as soon as you get back. The number one thing I got to say is I don't want to see you anymore, so don't try to get in touch with me. I thought we had something—like real love—but if you loved me, then how could you just go ahead and make me feel like this? I don't get why you acted like that. And it scares me. And number two is I let you do it and that scares me worse. You know what I mean? I mean I didn't want to make love to you that night, but I let you do it. For what? Like if I give you sex, you make sure I never have to be alone. Right? Like I been so lonely. So don't try and get in touch with me anyway.

And I'm not gonna see anybody else for a while, either. So there's no other guy, alright? I don't know why guys always think that—like we can't live without it. But if I start off lonely and end up feeling like dirt.... So, it's gonna be weird not having a boyfriend for a while. Or not having sex, anyway. Some people are gonna think I'm weird.

Number three is I really do love you. But not like I wanna get back together. Just like I really hope you work it out. And me too. Wish me luck. Sherri.

## *Flesh and Blood*

*JIM's room in the hospital. It's dimly lit and we can hear the sound of JIM's heart monitor. ALLAN enters.*

**ALLAN**    Jim? How ya doin'? It's Al.

Ya know what Ralph just said? He said I don't even know ya. What an asshole.

Like I know for instance that you wouldn't want to have your hair lookin' like that. What'd they cut it with anyway, a lawnmower?

*ALLAN checks his pockets.*

No comb, so I guess I can use my hands, eh?

*He rearranges JIM's hair, very gently.*

That's okay. Now you look a little bit more like yourself.

Ralph says you can still hear pretty good.

First thing I wanted to tell you is, I'm sorry I took off like that. But it was kind of a shock, eh? All at once. Sometimes I felt like you were with me, though. Nighttimes on the highway.

So your breathing's not too good, eh? That doesn't sound too comfortable.

It doesn't hurt, though, does it?

Ralph said… Ralph said he thought you wanted to talk to me. Prob'ly wanna chew me out, right?
All that shit I said about you killin' yourself and everything. It isn't true. I guess I was just… I dunno. Like back when I was in the hospital before? It wasn't exactly like I was tryin' to kill myself either. But they were right. It woulda been a pretty good accident.
So all of a sudden, it's like you're tellin' me you're just as stupid as I am. And I just got so pissed off.
But I know you were only tellin' me 'cause…. So that's okay, eh?

So I guess what I'm saying is, if it hurts too much to breathe an' that…

*Pause*

I know I haven't been visiting much, but it's not because I don't...

I'm just ashamed of myself, okay? You always took real good care o' me and then I turn around and treat you like shit. I guess that wasn't too mature. After what I said, callin' you a faggot an' that, I guess I figured I could never tell you how much I'm sorry. Well, I am. I'm sorry, Jimmy.

I know I'm not doin' such a great job, like o' being more responsible an' that. But I am tryin' though.

I guess what I'm trying to say is, if it hurts too much... um... you don't have to stick around just to take care o' me. I know you always wanted to be, like, my Dad an' that. And you been a real good Dad... You been a real good Dad. But now I can take care o' myself. Okay? So don't worry. I'm gettin' a lot better at takin' care of myself.

*Pause.*

You know what? I heard about people who said they saw lights and stuff. On the other side. And they saw people they knew there and it was like, really warm and everything? And they said that they felt, like—known, okay? Like people, or whoever was there—God or something—like he knew them and he loved them, okay?

I don't want it to hurt, okay? So if it hurts a lot, maybe you should just go wherever it is you're going. Okay? I'll hang around at this end and hold your hand until somebody grabs on on the other side. How's that?

Oh wait. Wait. I brought something.

*ALLAN takes his walkman from around his neck and slides the headset onto JIM. He puts the walkman on JIM's chest.*

Isn't that perfect? Perfect music. How many other brothers coulda taught me that?

I guess I never told you that I love you. But we knew that already, right?

Go ahead. I can take care of myself.

*As JIM stops breathing and the monitor stops, ALLAN takes several deep breaths.*

## *Flesh and Blood*

*Having changed into street clothes, JIM approaches the front of the stage. He's still in his first night at group. He listens to somebody else, then responds to them.*

**JIM**   Yeah. Okay. What I'm feeling in my body? Okay. A bit like throwing up, actually. An' I guess that's 'cause I was scared shitless about coming here tonight. Yeah. I had to put my hand on the door handle three times before I could open it. And then I just had to count to ten and do it. I never been involved in a gay organization before.

*He is interrupted.*

Well, I was in shock for about two months, but I think that's finally starting to turn around.

*Question.*

Well, it was... I was out for a walk with my friend Ralph. And we'd been having a pretty good day, actually. He hadn't been trying to get into my pants or anything, which is his favourite occupation. He's my ex. But he hadn't been trying to do that. So we were just walking along the sea wall and I started to get—I don't know if you ever get like this, but I started to hate the healthy. You know what I mean? Yah. So I was starting to hate the healthy, which takes a lot of energy, so we had to sit down. And then this little girl comes running along. Can't be more than about eighteen months. Not really talking yet. But she sees us and her face just lights up. Like we're the people she's been looking for all day. And then I notice that she's only got one and a half arms. Like her right arm is just this little flipper thing. And the fingers are like toes. But she doesn't care: they're wiggling away. And in a split second, I go from thinking, "Why me?" to "Why her?" What'd she ever do to anybody? And I'm just getting all fired up about this when her father comes running up to grab her. You know what his T-shirt says? "Shit happens." "Shit happens." It was like a revelation. Like these guys are a one-two punch from heaven. And then! And then! This is the weirdest part. This little kid says, "It isn't raining!" Just like that. "It isn't raining!" Like this is the secret we've all

been waiting for.
And she says it right to me.
Like we've all gotta live until we die, right?

*Question.*

I guess my biggest problem right now is guilt. Yeah. I told my mother. She's born again, right? I have a brother, too. I feel like... in my case, I just feel like I deserve it.

## *I Met a Bully on the Hill*
## by Martha Brooks and Maureen Hunter

*See Martha Brooks' biography on page 18.*

MAUREEN HUNTER is one of Canada's most successful playwrights. Her work has been produced extensively on Canada's major stages, as well as in Britain and the U.S. and on BBC and CBC Radio. It has been nominated for two Governor General's Awards and two Dora Mavor Moore Awards (Outstanding New Play). Her newest play, *Vinci*, premiered in 2002 at the National Arts Centre, Ottawa, in co-production with Manitoba Theatre Centre. It has since been produced at the Centaur in Montreal and at CanStage in Toronto. Other plays include *Transit of Venus*, *Atlantis*, *Footprints on the Moon* and *Beautiful Lake Winnipeg*.

ഗ   ഗ   ഗ

**Synopsis**

*I Met a Bully on the Hill* tells the story of 8-year-old J.J. (Jonquil Josephine) who has recently moved from the country to the city, leaving behind her beloved grandfather from whom she gets wise advice. She is befriended by DAVID, a quiet boy, with a great sense of humour and a passion for the trumpet, and by tough, good-hearted KARLA who doesn't let anyone push her around. Together the three friends attempt to deal with 9-year-old RAYMOND, the school bully, who extorts money from J.J. each time she uses "his hill."

The full script of *I Met a Bully on a Hill* is available through Scirocco Drama, an imprint of J. Gordon Shillingford Publishing, www.jgshillingford.com.

## I Met a Bully on the Hill

*The hill. A morning in late August. J.J. enters, dressed for school. In her hair is a yellow ribbon. She carries a knapsack with yellow trim and a coffee can with a plastic top, poked full of holes.*

**J.J.**  *(to audience)* Hi. My name's J.J. You might want to ask what that stands for but I'll tell you what. Don't! *(holds up can)* See this? There's a caterpillar inside and it's green with black stripes and yellow spots which makes it my favourite kind of caterpillar 'cause it's got yellow on it and yellow's my favourite colour. It's my lucky colour, too. As long as I wear yellow, nothing bad can happen.

*A shrill trumpet blast is heard, offstage. J.J. frowns, peers in the direction of the sound, shrugs, turns back to the audience.*

My grandpa gave me this caterpillar the day we moved—to keep me company now that I have to live in the city which I don't want to do but I have to anyway. My mum says I'll get used to it and even get to like it someday but I doubt it 'cause even after I got used to Brussels sprouts I didn't like them one bit. *(sighs)* But I have to try and like the city now that I live here 'cause I promised my grandpa I'd try real hard. He's the one who gave me this caterpillar—oh, I already told you that. He said if I took it to school on my first day, everybody would want to know something about me 'cause nobody knows anything about me now. I'm a stranger.

## I Met a Bully on the Hill

*The schoolyard. A week later, after school. DAVID enters, with his trumpet, and sits. He appears to be waiting for someone. Bored, he drums his fingers on his trumpet case. Then he opens the lid and reverently takes out the trumpet. He lifts it to his lips, takes a breath, closes his eyes and limbers up his fingers on the keys. He takes another breath. Beat. Sighs. Lowers the trumpet. Lifts the trumpet back to his lips, pretends to play a jazz standard, using his voice as the instrument. The choice of music can be up to the actor. The sound we hear is beautiful, soulful and unexpected—the real DAVID. It reveals his love for music and his longing to be really good. Towards the end of his song, J.J. straggles in, wearing lots of yellow. She stops and listens.*

**J.J.**   Wow!

*Embarrassed, DAVID fumbles with his trumpet and quickly puts it back in its case.*

I've never heard anything like that. You know what that's like? That's like at night when you stand on the best hill in the country and a million summer stars all fall around you.

**DAVID**   That's how I want to play my trumpet someday. I don't know if I ever will.

**J.J.**   You will.

**DAVID**   Maybe.

**J.J.**   Of course you will. *(pause)* What are you doing here?

**DAVID**   I was waiting for you.

**J.J.**   You were?

**DAVID**   I was. You're famous.

**J.J.**   Sure.

**DAVID**   You are. You've got the class record. Four detentions in one week. Impressive.

**J.J.**   Yeah. Want my autograph?

*J.J. sits cross-legged on the ground, throws her books down beside her, drops her forehead onto one hand.*

**DAVID**    What's wrong? What did I say? Are you mad? You're crying. Why are you crying? *(sits next to her, puts an arm around her)* Hey, I was just teasing.

**J.J.**    *(sobs)* I know.

**DAVID**    *(He pats her shoulder awkwardly.)* Go ahead and cry, you'll feel better. But watch this shirt. No, no, just kidding. You go ahead and cry all over it. Get it real wet. You'd be doing me a big favour. I hate this shirt. I really hate it. I told my mum I wanted a classy striped shirt like Wynton Marsalis wears? What does she come home with? *(pulls out the bottom)* A wimp shirt. Look at it!

**J.J.**    I hate this school! I hate everybody here. I want to go back to the country. Everything was nice there. I had everything I ever wanted in the country. The people I knew were nice. They liked me.

**DAVID**    *(pats her back vigorously)* Well, I like you. *(stands)* Are you feeling better now?

**J.J.**    I don't belong here. I don't fit in. When I was in the country, I never had to worry about what would happen when I went out the door. *(pause)* Except when I was six and my grandpa had these three White Rock roosters and they used to wait for me at the foot of the hill and when I came home from school they'd chase me all the way back up the hill and bite at the backs of my legs. It was really scary and that was just after my dad died which made it worse 'cause I felt like I had to act like a big girl so my mum wouldn't worry about me, but she did anyway.

**DAVID**    Gee.

**J.J.**    Then one day I came running up the hill with those stupid roosters chasing after me and I looked up and there was my grandpa laughing and laughing. I was so mad at him I started to cry. And then he picked me up and gave me a big hug and told me if I'd just learn to see what's funny in things I wouldn't be so scared. Easy for him to say. *(pause)* I wish my grandpa was here now. He'd know what to do.

**DAVID**   You mean about Raymond.

**J.J.**   Yeah.

**DAVID**   Know what we call him behind his back?

**J.J.**   What?

**DAVID**   *(slowly, gleefully)* Poop-Along.

**J.J.**   Poop-Along!

**DAVID**   Because he is one. He's been the biggest poop around, ever since he failed Grade Three. He's been mean to just about everyone all summer.

**J.J.**   I thought it was just me.

Andrew Massingham in *The General*, 1986.

## *A Secret Life* by Edward Roy

EDWARD ROY's various activities as a theatre practitioner include directing, writing, dramaturgy, acting and teaching. He is a recipient of The Pauline McGibbon Award for Directing, a Chalmers Award for Playwriting, two Dora Awards for outstanding production and the Harold Alternative Theatre Award, along with various other nominations. He is currently the Artistic Director of Topological Theatre, Company Dramaturg/Associate Artist at Buddies in Bad Times Theatre and Training Coordinator at the Workman Arts Centre for Addiction and Mental Health.

∽ ∽ ∽

### Synopsis

DOUG MCGRATH lives in a world of disillusionment with no promise of a productive and fulfilling future. Due to economic instability and family strife, he has moved often in his sixteen years and has attended many different schools. Once again, he is in a new neighbourhood, at a new school, and with a new peer group. Despite the difficulties, DOUG has grown accustomed to reinventing himself each time. *A Secret Life* begins in the moments before DOUG has to face the choice of another new school or giving up.

The full script of *A Secret Life* is available through Playwrights Guild of Canada, www.playwrightsguild.ca.

## *A Secret Life*

**SUSAN**     Sometimes it can be so hard to get to know someone. Like Doug... I've been watching him around school. I've never seen him hang out or talk with anybody. That could be because he hasn't been here that long but I get the feeling that there's something bothering him. He has such sad eyes... sad eyes... even though I don't really know him I'd like to help him if I could. Isn't that weird? Having feelings for someone you don't even know? So today he was sitting alone in the cafeteria and I walked up to him and pretended I needed to talk to him about our art project. He hardly said a word. Then I told him if he didn't feel like talking right now we could always get together after school sometime and go somewhere and talk. I practically asked him for a date. Then he gets even more quiet, mumbles something about going for a job interview and leaves. What can I say? It was weird. But I'm not giving up. We're still working together on the project and sooner or later I'm going to find out what's going on.

## A Secret Life

**ANDY**   When I first met Doug I thought he was a total loser. Acting like Mr. Bad Attitude. I thought for sure me and Susan would get stuck doing most of the work on this ourselves. Actually I was hoping it would work out that way. It would've given me some time to be alone with her again and maybe convince her to give us another chance. We were going out for two months and broke up a month and a half ago because she said she didn't want to get too serious. She said I was too possessive. So maybe I did get a little jealous when she talked to other guys but that's what girls like isn't it? We've both been dating other people but neither of us has met anyone special so I thought it was just a matter of time… but then Doug shows up. He's got money. Great ideas. And just my luck he turns out to be OK. After all he's saving my butt by doing most of the work on this project. Susan's totally into him. I guess I was wrong about the guy. Susan and me are never going to get back together again. I would've never guessed that he was rich. Hey, I wonder if he'll lend me twenty bucks until Monday?

## *A Secret Life*

**MISS LIN**   I can't tell you how frustrating this is. I didn't really think Doug's life was as together as he pretended. I can't expect Doug to open up when we're just getting to know each other but I am pretty close to some of my students; they know I'd never discuss anything personal they tell me with another teacher like it was just another piece of gossip. But it takes time to build that kind of trust. When I was in high-school I had a problem... drugs.... My parents were very success oriented... and I thought that secretly they cared more about my marks then they did about me. Before I started high-school I was a total over achiever, but once I got there I started to hang out with a gang that didn't think it was cool to get the highest marks. It was much cooler to hang out and get high. So I spent the first two years juggling failing grades, angry parents, and trying every drug that went in front of my nose. But it caught up with me. I was taking an English exam, high on speed and acid, just staring out the window. Everything seemed a million miles away and I felt incredibly lonely. Then all of a sudden I didn't want to be stoned anymore but there was nothing I could do about it. I started to panic. Then I got hysterical. My parents had to pick me up at the hospital. Eventually we worked everything out. So when I became a teacher I promised myself that I would be available to any student who wanted to talk. Maybe if someone would have been able to see that I was having problems and tried to help me I wouldn't have had to go through so much pain. And sometimes if you want to help you have to bend the rules a little because it would be a real shame if Doug just fell through the cracks.

## *A Secret Life*

*DOUG sleeps on the street.*

**DOUG**    *(voiceover)* Where am I supposed to go? That's what I'd like to know. I mean you don't have to be a genius to figure out that living on the street isn't life in the fast lane. Can't get a job cause there aren't any. I'm screwed. Nowhere to go. *(DOUG speaks.)* But I'm not going back home tonight. No way. It'll just be the same crap. We'll end up yelling at each other all night. You know she wouldn't be half as freaked out if the TV was working. My old lady watches TV twenty-four hours a day. Tabloids, talkshows, soaps, you name it. Sometimes she turns it on before she even wakes up like she had it surgically attached to her hand or something. That's where she goes when she wants to escape. I read somewhere that TV is the Pablum of the masses. I always hated Pablum. I stopped watching it when I realized that I was never going to have the kind of life that most people on TV programs have. No nice house. No cutesy neighbours. No escape. One time after we had a fight I hid the control on her. She got up one morning and it wasn't there. She walked around the house like she lost her best friend. She looked everywhere. Then she started to yell. So I gave the remote back to her. She didn't say anything. She just hit me. Now the TV's broken and we can't afford to get it fixed. Her "medication" isn't helping her. No escape. Nowhere to go. Just like me. Trapped.

photo by Ian Chrysler

Clare Preuss in *Andrew's Tree*, 1990.

## Girl Who Loved Her Horses
## by Drew Hayden Taylor

*See Drew Hayden Taylor's biography on page 26.*

ട്ട     ട്ട     ട്ട

**Synopsis**

RALPH, a young Native man, remembers the time when he, his sister SHELLEY and their friend WILLIAM sat around their kitchen table and discussed their mother's new idea—the Everything Wall. She had started the Everything Wall so that anyone living on or near the reserve could come to their home and contribute an idea, a story or a drawing.

DANIELLE, a young girl who lives on the wrong side of the tracks, wants to have a turn at the Everything Wall. She draws a magnificent stallion that seems to be everything DANIELLE is not; strength, confidence, freedom and power. The young friends, WILLIAM, RALPH and SHELLEY are amazed by the power of the drawing and begin to take notice of DANIELLE. Through changes in her drawing of the horse DANIELLE is able to express her feelings and finds a way to communicate with them.

The full script of *Girl Who Loved Her Horses* is available from Talonbooks, www.talonbooks.com.

## Girl Who Loved Her Horses

*SHELLEY goes to investigate the door, she pulls it open to reveal DANIELLE standing there, looking smaller than ever.*

**SHELLEY**   Who are you?

*DANIELLE, the poster girl for shyness, doesn't respond. The other kids look, surprised to see her.*

**WILLIAM**   *(secretly to RALPH)* Oh man, Ralph, look who it is. The dumb girl.

**RALPH**   She's not dumb.

**WILLIAM**   Sure acts like it sometimes.

**SHELLEY**   Aren't you gonna say something?

**RALPH**   She doesn't talk much. Doesn't do much of anything.

*DANIELLE just stands there, looking more and more like the proverbial shrinking violet.*

**SHELLEY**   Well, you coming in?

*DANIELLE hesitates for a moment.*

What are you afraid of? I said "come in."

*DANIELLE manages to enter the kitchen.*

**RALPH**   Hey, Danielle.

**SHELLEY**   Danielle, that's a pretty name. I was thinking of changing my name to Kateri—you know, after the Indian saint—when I got older. Better than Shelley. So what do you want, kid?

*DANIELLE mumbles something but it's impossible to make it out.*

Tell me, I won't bite.

**WILLIAM**   Don't believe it.

*DANIELLE struggles to speak louder.*

**DANIELLE**   I heard you could draw here.

**SHELLEY**    Yeah, do you wanna?

*DANIELLE shyly nods her head.*

Well, okay, the pencil crayons are over there. There's still a lot of room left, big space over there. *(pointing)* That's my house there, don't you just love the tulips? I saw this house once when we went to the city. That's where I want to live when I get out of school. So draw what you want, my mom gives a prize every Monday night to the best picture. She won't tell us what the prize is though. And then she washes it off for Tuesday. Okay?

**DANIELLE**    Thank you.

*DANIELLE shyly approaches "The Everything Wall." She walks around the card players and tries to reach the pencil crayons but they are too high for her. She jumps up but still can't reach them.*

**WILLIAM**    Will you hurry up, Shelley, it's your turn.

*SHELLEY grabs the pencils and gives them to her.*

**SHELLEY**    Here. *(to RALPH)* Did you watch him? He didn't cheat did he?

**DANIELLE**    *(in an unnoticed voice)* Thank you.

*She examines her pencils closely, and removes five specific colours. The others she puts on the counter. She stands there and looks at the wall.*

**SHELLEY**    Danielle? You live around here?

**DANIELLE**    My mom and I live across the tracks.

**SHELLEY**    Oh, so you aren't part of the Reserve?

**DANIELLE**    No.

**SHELLEY**    Who's your mom?

**WILLIAM**    Elsie Fiddler.

*SHELLEY reacts to that. It does not look like good news. She speaks in hushed tones.*

**SHELLEY**    Ohh. You in her class?

**RALPH**    Yeah but that's about it. We don't hang around with her or anything. I don't think I've ever seen her hang out with anybody.

**SHELLEY**    No friends? Do you guys pick on her or tease her?

**WILLIAM**    No, you've got to have a personality to be picked on.

**SHELLEY**    What?

**WILLIAM**    Something for people to make fun of. She doesn't have enough to tease.

**RALPH**    She's sort of like a shadow.

**WILLIAM**    Just a dull blob, not making any noise or drawing attention to herself.

**SHELLEY**    Oh how sad.

**WILLIAM**    Yeah I guess, can we get back to the game now?

*SHELLEY, WILLIAM and RALPH focus on the card game completely unaware of DANIELLE and what she's about to go through. DANIELLE puts pencil crayon to wall and the HORSE comes through the wall slowly. He is skittish around her, checking out his space. She moves toward him. He looks slightly dangerous, but she's not afraid.*

*The HORSE glows with energy, radiating everything that DANIELLE isn't. It has strength, confidence, freedom. Power. DANIELLE slowly, carefully continues to approach the HORSE. She reaches out, her hands desperate to touch him, and at the same time afraid he'll disappear the moment they make contact. He swings her around, fast and amazing at first, then tenderly. She slides down the front of the HORSE slowly, her back against him, her face glowing. She makes a huge sound of joy and release. She laughs and giggles like the child she has a right to be.*

**DANIELLE**    I knew you'd be there. I knew it.

*She closes her eyes, still radiant. The HORSE slips away from her and back through the wall. She turns to find him gone.*

*There is a moment of sadness as she allows the power to leave her. She goes towards the wall.*

*A large, magnificent creation of the HORSE is on the wall. DANIELLE puts the last touch on her creation and then neatly puts the remaining pencil crayons back into the package.*

**SHELLEY**   Ralph, I think he was cheating but I don't know how.

**WILLIAM**   *(cocky)* Too fast for you, huh?

**DANIELLE**   Thank you.

*She exits.*

**RALPH**   So you were cheating!

**WILLIAM**   I never said that. You can't prove it.

*Upset, SHELLEY throws her cards on the table and storms away. She is the first to see the HORSE.*

**SHELLEY**   Uh guys...

*The two boys follow SHELLEY's line of sight and see the HORSE. They get up to get a better view. They all stand there, eyes wide, amazed and silent for a few moments.*

**RALPH**   Nice horse!

**SHELLEY**   Amazing!

**WILLIAM**   Ultra-amazing! That was Danielle, wasn't it?

*They all approach the wall, RALPH reaches out and touches the wall to make sure it's real.*

**SHELLEY**   That shy little girl....

**WILLIAM**   It's almost like it's alive. Where'd she learn that!?

**RALPH**   Not with our art teacher. I think it's looking at me.

**SHELLEY**   This can't be painted over. It would be a sin, like painting over the Sixteen chapel.

**RALPH**   That's Sistine Chapel.

**SHELLEY**   A sin's a sin Ralph, no matter what you call it. I think I want to look at this every day.

**WILLIAM**    Gotta admit, it is beautiful.

**SHELLEY**    I'll ask Mom if we can keep it.

*The three stand there and look at it for a ridiculously long time.*

**RALPH**    Nice horse.

**WILLIAM**    I'm not gonna win, am I?

*In unison, RALPH and SHELLEY shake their heads, their eyes never leaving the HORSE.*

## *Little Sister* by Joan MacLeod

JOAN MACLEOD is a Vancouver-based writer who spent seven seasons with Tarragon Theatre in Toronto where she premiered four plays. All of her plays have been performed extensively across Canada, Britain and the U.S. She is also a poet and prose writer. Her work has been translated into five languages.

*ς     ς     ς*

### Synopsis

*Little Sister* begins at the start of the school year, where we find KATIE in a new school, following a move due to her parents' divorce. She spends her lunch-times with TRACEY and BELLA in the washroom of their school where they discuss everything— school, boys, clothes, weight and how to solve their seemingly insurmountable problems. The pressures begin to build when KATIE is paired with JAY, (who has a relationship with TRACEY) in science class and they must learn to work together. Life seems to unravel for the five characters after KATIE collapses in class and is hospitalized for anorexia.

The full script of *Little Sister* is available from Talonbooks, www.talonbooks.com.

## *Little Sister*

**KATIE**    Dear Dad. I am feeling much, much better. I am sorry you cancelled your trip to Costa Rica. Don't worry about me! everyone here says I'm doing fine. They are all very proud of me.

*KATIE tears up the paper, she is furious, out of bed, pacing.*

I make lunch, make lunch for me and Buddy and Andrew. Mummy's little helper. I put six slices of bread on the counter, *six*. The bread is soft and big and brown. I cover the bread with peanut butter because I *love love love* peanut butter. I slice up bananas and put them on top. Then four hey-dey cookies apiece into little plastic bags *and* one big red apple for me.

I *don't* jog to school. I get a ride with Mum but I make her let me out a block before so no one will see I'm with her. I study right until the bell.

I always eat lunch in the girls' washroom, always sit under the Tampax machine. I've never had a period and think by sitting under the machine this will somehow help. I realize this is not very logical but to the best of my knowledge I am the only girl in grade ten who hasn't started. I take the sandwich apart. I scrape all the peanut butter off the little slices of banana and eat them slowly. I eat the crusts, I *love* crusts. I don't even look at the cookies, I keep them hidden inside the bag and then I throw the bag into the trash. Let's do lunch.

The last class of the day is history. On my way to class I feel clear as spring water, clear as glass, when I move through the halls, I am moving in a glass box. I take my seat. When I leave there will be no impressions, no trace of me. I put my hands around my waist because my stomach is crying.

Slides of the Holocaust. There is no way of knowing who lived or died. Who are the survivors? I am feeling badly for the victims of Auschwitz as is the rest of my class but I am more concerned about the four hey-dey cookies in my brown recycled lunch bag in the trash.

I want to dive through to the bottom, dive into the thrown-out sandwiches, butts, damp paper towels, apple cores and surface with *my lunch*, a giant pearl I can stuff inside and swallow and swallow...

*Don't.* I am afraid of the sound of my stomach, afraid my bones make noise inside my skin when I walk up the aisle but I am *most* afraid because the inside of my mouth tastes like peanut butter and *it should not.*

*KATIE breaks down, curls up on her bed.*

*Somebody!... Listen!* Help me please!

I'm hungry! I am so hungry...

photo by *Andrew Oxenham*

Erin Shields (left), Soraya Peerbaye (centre) and Michelle Polak in *Martian Summer*, 2002.

## *Bang Boy Bang!* by Edward Roy

*See Edward Roy's biography on page 40.*

§ § §

### Synopsis

*Bang Boy Bang!* is a dramatic monologue. In the opening scene ROD CLARK, a teenager, wakes up hung over and listens to his phone messages. One of the messages is from a young woman accusing him of date rape. Confused and unable to recall the events of the night before, ROD must piece together exactly what happened. Presented in a unique multi-media style, this play deals with the hard realities of dating, intimacy, emotions, impulses and peer pressure.

The full script of *Bang Boy Bang!* is available from Playwrights Guild of Canada, www.playwrightsguild.ca.

## *Bang Boy Bang!*

**ROD**    *(live)* So girls fantasize about guys, big news. I still think guys and girls live in two different worlds and there's no way of knowing what their world is really like and I'm not about to get a sex change to find out. You know what I'm talking about? Of course you don't, you don't have any trouble talking to girls at all. But whenever I try to talk to one a little voice in my head begins to say things.

*ROD's face appears on the projection screen.*

*(on screen)* Are you really stupid enough to think that she's going to be interested in anything you have to say? The shirt you're wearing makes you look like a dork. It's too late to turn around now, she knows you're walking up to her. That's why she's got that, "I hope he's not going to talk to me" look in her eyes. Don't fake a smile, your teeth are yellow. Relax, your shoulders are up to your ears. I forgot what I was going to say.

*The image of ROD dissolves from the screen.*

**TAYLOR**    *(voiceover)* Get a grip, Rod, you're going squirrely. You worry too much about it.

**ROD**    *(live)* Well I don't have to worry about it anymore because none of the girls would be caught dead talking to Mr. Disease.

**TAYLOR**    Hey before you know it everybody will forget that you were the guy who caught a disease but they'll still remember that you're not a virgin. And neither am I.

**ROD**    *(live)* What?

**TAYLOR**    This weekend at Greg's party—you remember what a party is right? Or have you been grounded so long that you've forgotten?

**ROD**    *(voiceover)* Not funny.

**TAYLOR**    Anyway last week at Greg's party I met this girl... I think her name was Wendy.

*Ambient music: sensual with a hint of malevolence begins to play. Abstract images alluding to moving flesh begin to appear on the projection screen as TAYLOR continues.*

*TAYLOR remains talking on voiceover as the music and images play.*

She's a friend of Greg's sister. Anyway everybody was dancing in the front room and I went to the kitchen to get another beer and I met her in the hallway. She was standing there alone and I thought she was really cute so I started talking to her. She was really drunk. So was I but not as drunk as her. She was laughing at everything I said. She finally laughed so hard she fell on the floor. Then somehow I ended up on the floor laughing with her. I don't know how long we were on the floor laughing but when we finally stopped she looked at me and then she kissed me. Man she was wild. She started jamming her tongue down my throat right from the word go. In like two seconds we were rolling all over the hallway floor. It was getting so hot I decided to drag her up to Greg's room. You've been to Greg's place before haven't you? It's on the second floor of their house. We could barely hear the noise from the party downstairs. God this Wendy chick was so drunk she could barely hear herself think never mind the party downstairs. So I just pushed her toward the bed and continued the make-out party. Once I had her on the bed I knew I could make my move. This was one opportunity I wasn't going to miss. I mean she was totally blotto and raring to go so I started to undo her top... and then she started to get all nervous or something.... So I told her to relax and I just kept going...

*As the music and abstract images continue, on the projection screen WENDY's text is superimposed moving slowly across the screen.*

**WENDY**     *(projected text)* No don't...

**TAYLOR**     I could tell she was really getting into what she was doing because she really started to squirm.

**WENDY**     *(projected text)* Stop it...

**TAYLOR**     She was pretending she wanted me to stop...

**WENDY**     (*projected text*) Please... don't...

**TAYLOR**     But I was too into it to stop if you know what
I mean...

**WENDY**     (*projected text*) Stop...

**TAYLOR**     Come on don't you like it?

**WENDY**     (*projected text*) I don't want to do this... I said no...
please... stop...

> *The images on the screen and the music fades out.*

**TAYLOR**     It was fantastic. I had no idea that getting laid would
feel so great. We didn't talk much after we were finished. She
just got real quiet and lay there on the bed with her face in
the pillow. I think she just wanted to sleep it off. Like you
said, girls can be so hard to figure out eh? I mean after she
starts the whole necking thing in the hallway and then goes
up to the bedroom with me she pretends she doesn't want to
do it anymore. She started to say no I don't want to a couple
of times but I knew she really meant yes because if she didn't
really want to then she would've said something after we had
done it. But she didn't say a word she just buried her face in
the pillow. Take it from me, Rod, no doesn't always mean no.
Girls like to do it just as much as we do only they're not
supposed to admit it, so most of the time they say no because
they don't want to look like sluts. So they kind of expect us to
be able to know when they say no they really mean... yes.
I can't wait until I get a chance to do it again, cause I want to
bang, boy bang!

**ROD**     (*live*) Yeah well no chance of that happening to me
because my parents aren't going to let me have a social life
until I'm eighteen.

**TAYLOR**     Sooner or later your luck has got to change.

> *A school bell rings and we hear the sound of a classroom full of
> students.*

## *Bang Boy Bang!*

*We hear LAURA on voiceover.*

**LAURA**   So how are you finding the party? Are you enjoying it?

**ROD**   *(live)* Yes. Only now the party seemed like it was a million miles away and I couldn't stop smiling.

**LAURA**   We should go downstairs and join the party.

**ROD**   Just one more kiss.

**LAURA**   One kiss.

**ROD**   *(live)* She kissed me again and something changed inside me. We were melting together and I didn't want it to stop. I just wanted to touch her everywhere…

We were both breathing heavy… and I knew, I could tell that she was as excited as I was…

**LAURA**   We're missing the party.

**ROD**   *(live)* Then everything sped up twice as fast and I wasn't thinking anymore. I was just reacting to this electricity that went zapping through me every time I kissed her or touched her skin… and I knew she liked it too.

**LAURA**   I'm feeling a little dizzy, we better stop.

**ROD**   *(live)* Don't you like what we're doing?

**LAURA**   Sure I like it…

**ROD**   *(live)* I didn't stop…

**LAURA**   Rod…

**ROD**   *(live)* I couldn't stop…

**LAURA**   Rod no…

**ROD**   *(live)* Oh come on, come on doesn't it feel good? Doesn't it?

**LAURA**   Please Rod I want to stop…

**ROD**   *(live)* Shhhhh… shhhh! I could hear her clothes ripping and she was trying to push me away but I couldn't stop. My voice sounded like it belonged to somebody else. "You said

you liked how it felt didn't you?" I was on top of her...
I don't remember how that happened... but she was
underneath me and I was holding her arms down.

**LAURA**  Noooo!

**ROD**  *(live)* No doesn't always mean no... no can mean yes...
I want it to mean yes... but it didn't... not when Laura said
it... screamed it... screamed it so loud in my ear that I shot up
off of her and saw somebody standing on the other side of the
room looking at me with his shirt undone and his pants
falling off his hips. It was me. I was seeing myself in a mirror
across the room and I didn't recognize myself. The face that
was looking back at me was wild and angry... I was angry...
angry because I was torn away from something I wanted...
something I needed... then I looked at the other stranger
behind me in the mirror on the bed. It was Laura but she
didn't look like Laura anymore.

**LAURA**  I'm not afraid of you.

**ROD**  *(live)* What are you talking about? Why should you be
afraid of me? We were just having fun. Weren't we?! Jeezz, it's
just like Taylor said, you girls like it just as much as we do
but you pretend you don't. You were enjoying it, I know you
were. She didn't say anything. She just looked back at me and
began to cry and I felt cheated. I wanted to shake her until
she stopped. Then I ran. Ran from that bedroom down the
hall into a wall of people. They weren't there earlier, were
they? Did they hear her scream?

**TAYLOR**  *(on tape)* They kind of expect us to be able to know
when they say no that they really mean... yes. I can't wait
until I get a chance to do it again, cause all I want to do is
bang boy, bang.

**ROD**  *(live)* That's all I wanted to do, that's all my whole body
wanted to do—and everything inside me said yes! Yes this is
going to happen the way I want it to, so I can remember....
Remember it, doing it, feeling it, touching it, tasting it....
I wanted to be so different from the first time. This time
I wanted to be in control. But I wasn't.... In my whole life
nobody told me this could happen... that I could lose control

'cause I wanted something so badly—so badly—that I could shut out the parts of my heart and brain that were telling what I was doing was wrong. All I could feel was the heat burning inside me when I touched Laura, until it roared like a fire through me, and the fire was out of control. And now I know that fire burns in me, and Arthur, and Taylor, and... everybody. And it can turn into a fireball. A fireball I don't want to remember.

Kimwun Perehenic and Matthew McFadzean in *Pop Song*, 2000.

photo by *David Hawe*

## *Buncha Young Artists Having Their Say*

In 2000 and 2002, Theatre Direct mounted the ambitious Buncha' Young Artists havin' their say... Festivals. Eight new works were premiered as full productions and played in repertoire to young audiences and the general public at the Theatre Passe Muraille backspace. While each piece is distinct in subject matter and style, they all share an unfettered courageousness in their willingness to grapple with difficult and controversial subject matter. The festival and the productions caught the attention of the critics and garnered rave reviews for the writing and performances. We have chosen selections from both festivals.

## *Pop Song* by Sean Reycraft

SEAN REYCRAFT was born in Glencoe, Ontario. His plays include *One Good Marriage, Stranger Things Happen* and *Roundabout*. For *Pop Song*, Reycraft won the Chalmers Canadian Play Award (Theatre for Young Audiences). *Pop Song* has been adapted into a short film, and premiered at the 2003 Toronto International Film Festival.

ဢ   ဢ   ဢ

**Synopsis**

*Pop Song* is about Stewart and Steph, two 13-year-olds so obsessed with the silly, meaningless dramas of their relationship that they're completely unprepared for the realities of it—with tragic consequences.

The full script of *Pop Song* is available from Playwrights Guild of Canada, www.playwrightsguild.ca.

## Pop Song

*January. Four months.*

**ANNOUNCER**   So Christmas was a mess, New Year's felt old and now you've got the January blahs? Who doesn't! That's why we've got the January Hula this Friday! We're crankin' up the heat in the gym and fillin' the floor with sand—so forget your shoes, wear your short shorts and prepare to feel tropical!

*STACEY dances apart from STEVE. She pays no attention to him.*

**STACEY**   I'm not talkin' to you.

**STEVE**   Fine.

**STACEY**   Go sit somewheres else.

**STEVE**   Why won't you call me back?

**STACEY**   I said I'm not talkin'—

**STEVE**   Won't look at me in the hall—

**STACEY**   Shut-up Steve just shut it.

**STEVE**   —won't sit with me at lunch—

**STACEY**   Stand. Over there.

**STEVE**   —won't smoke between classes—

**STACEY**   Stop talkin' don't talk again.

**STEVE**   —won't listen when I TALK—

**STACEY**   I hate you you're not good.

**STEVE**   Now you're cryin'.

**STACEY**   TWO WEEKS you were alone.

**STEVE**   Two weeks is a long time.

**STACEY**   I DIDN'T WANNA GO.

**STEVE**   Didn't want to but you did.

**STACEY**   So's when I get back—

**STEVE**   You went without me.

**STACEY**   —I hear all around the school—

**STEVE**   You left me alone.

**STACEY**    —everybody almost runnin' to tell me—

**STEVE**    I was mad at you.

**STACEY**    SO'S YOU'RE KISSIN' CATHY COAD ON NEW YEAR'S EVE.

**STEVE**    Just kissin' that's all.

**STACEY**    IN PEG SHAW'S BATHTUB.

**STEVE**    Stop cryin'.

**STACEY**    No.

**STEVE**    People're lookin'.

**STACEY**    No.

**STEVE**    You wanna break up?

**STACEY**    I'm mad at you.

**STEVE**    Break up for good?

>    *Pause.*

**STACEY**    No.

**STEVE**    'Cause I don't.

**STACEY**    You don't?

**STEVE**    No.

**STACEY**    Don't kiss her again.

**STEVE**    Don't leave me again.

**STACEY**    Don't touch her again.

**STEVE**    Don't go away again.

**STACEY**    Don't look at her no more.

**STEVE**    She's right over there.

**STACEY**    STEVE.

**STEVE**    I don't like bein' away from you.

**STACEY**    I don't wanna be without you.

**STEVE**    We're not breakin' up.

**STACEY**    We're never breakin' up.

**STEVE**    I'm glad you're back.

**STACEY**    I love you, Stevie.

**STEVE**    Right.

## *Pop Song*

**ANNOUNCER**     Attention all students: thanks to fundraising we've managed to drop the cost of Prom tickets to a measly twenty bucks! Twenty bucks! That's all it costs to bid "good-bye" to our graduating class and wish them a great future! So wear your finest and grab a date 'cause this night's gonna be *classic*!

> *STACEY and STEVE arrive dressed for the Grad. STACEY stands in humiliation.*

**STACEY**     Every girl here's prettier than me.

**STEVE**     Not every one.

**STACEY**     STEVE.

**STEVE**     I'm payin' you a compliment.

**STACEY**     I'm supposed to be the prettiest.

**STEVE**     I like your dress.

**STACEY**     You do?

**STEVE**     I do.

**STACEY**     *(pain)* Ow.

**STEVE**     What?

**STACEY**     OW.

**STEVE**     What is it?

**STACEY**     I think I ate too much before comin'.

**STEVE**     It's nothin'.

**STACEY**     Else I ate somethin' bad.

**STEVE**     Glad I brought chips.

**STACEY**     Why's it hurt like this?

**STEVE**     All they got here's vegetables and stupid dip.

**STACEY**     Dance with me.

**STEVE**     Don't like this music.

**STACEY**    Request somethin' then.

**STEVE**    Request?

**STACEY**    They let you do that at the Grad.

**STEVE**    What'll I request?

**STACEY**    Whatever you want. But you have to dedicate it.

**STEVE**    To who?

**STACEY**    The graduates.

**STEVE**    I don't like the graduates.

**STACEY**    Dedicate it to me then—*AH!*

**STEVE**    What d'you want to hear?

**STACEY**    Anything you want.

**STEVE**    What do I want to hear?

**STACEY**    I have to sit down.

*STACEY collapses into a nearby chair.*

**STEVE**    You're sittin' down at a dance?

**STACEY**    I hafta.

**STEVE**    You? Sit?

**STACEY**    I'm not feelin' so good.

**STEVE**    I'm goin' to request somethin'.

**STACEY**    OK.

**STEVE**    Hold my chips.

**STACEY**    Yeah.

**STEVE**    Stace?

**STACEY**    What?

**STEVE**    You're the prettiest.

**STACEY**    Thanks.

*STEVE goes.*

*(pain worsening)* Stevie? Stevie? Stevie? *(really worsening)*
Stevie Stevie      Stevie Stevie STEVIE STEVIE STEVIE
STEVIE AAHHHHHH—

**STEVE**   Stace?

**STACEY**   Steve—

**STEVE**   That was easy.

**STACEY**   *(struggling up)* I wanna go.

**STEVE**   What?

**STACEY**   I hafta go.

> *STEVE's grabbed onto STACEY's hand. He pulls her back to stay.*

**STEVE**   Why?

**STACEY**   Can't stay.

**STEVE**   I requested a song.

**STACEY**   Please.

**STEVE**   He's playin' it next.

**STACEY**   Please.

**STEVE**   Listen.

**STACEY**   Please Steve—

**STEVE**   Here Stace—

**STACEY**   AH my God—

**STEVE**   This is for you.

> *The music stops. There's a spotlight on STACEY.*

**STACEY**   *(without emotion)* I run I run I run I run outta the gym
down the hall past Nina Webster past Mr. Robinson past Jake
Fischer PUSH OPEN the double glass door so heavy and into
the washroom first stall locked second stall open but too close
to the first so it's the THIRD THEN slam the door shut lock it
tight lift UP my dress ALL THE WAY up and over pullin'
down my pantyhose pushin' down my pantyhose pushin'

down my underwear— (*Screaming.*) AAAAAAHHHH HHH-
HHHHHHM!

**STEVE**    (*repeated under and slightly behind*) I run I run I run
I follow outta the gym down the hall past Nina Webster past
Mr. Robinson past Jake Fischer PUSH OPEN the double glass
door so heavy and into the washroom first stall locked second
stall open but too close to the first so it's the THIRD THEN
slam the door you locked it tight you lift UP your dress so
pretty your dress your dress ALL THE WAY up and over
pullin' down your pantyhose pushin' down your underwear—

> *STACEY lets go of STEVE's hand causing him to fall back.*

(*panicked*) STACEY? STACEY? STACEY?—STACE? YOU
ALRIGHT?

> *STACEY stops and stares out.*

**STACEY**    (*with no emotion*) Fine.

**STEVE**    STACE, YOU OKAY?

**STACEY**    You bet.

**STEVE**    STACE WHAT'S THE PROBLEM???

**STACEY**    (*looking down*) What's the problem?

**STEVE**    STACE???

> *STACEY looks up again saying nothing. Blackout.*

photo by Andrew Oxenham

Marjorie Chan in *The Phoenix Rides a Skateboard*, 2002.

## *Vicious Little Boyz in the Rain* by Gil Garratt

GIL GARRATT is a theatre artist in Toronto, primarily an actor and playwright but also a director and designer. Though he has been writing plays professionally for several years now, Garratt has been secretly writing poems for over a decade. He is currently the Associate Artistic Director at the Blyth Festival, Blyth, Ontario.

§   §   §

### Synopsis

The Boyz, BUZZARD, FREAK, STOOPID and RAIN (who is actually a girl) are "colourful urban primitives" or social "scavengers" who believe that the only means to achieving utopia, known as CaliNova, is anarchy. As such, the foundation of their hierarchical group structure is built upon rules that challenge the existence of humanity and love. Void of tenderness and filled with rage, the Boyz embark upon a volatile journey, destroying everything in their path. But, along the way, BUZZARD, STOOPID and RAIN discover that the power of love cannot be denied. By learning to turn a compassionate hand to the world, they take a proactive stand and realize that one person can make a difference.

The full script for *Vicious Little Boyz in the Rain* is available from Theatre Direct.

## Vicious Little Boyz in the Rain

*FREAK laughs then joins in. Boy games. BUZZ stares after
RAIN with the binoculars, for awhile. He then turns and stares
in awe at the boyz. They are airplanes, getting ready to take off,
over the sound system comes the roaring sound of old warplane
propellers.*

**BUZZ**   *(screaming over the sound)* WHAT CHA DOIN?

**FREAK**   WHAT?

**STOOPID**   *(to Freak)* WHAT'S HE SAYING?

**BUZZ**   WHAT CHAS DOIN?

**FREAK**   Oh. AIR RAID.

*STOOPID and FREAK take off, swooping at each other and the
audience, dropping red paint bombs at the ground and screaming. BUZZ laughs and then joins in, FREAK and BUZZ tear
offstage through the audience. STOOPID then runs, crashes
and slides on his knees stopping at the very edge of the stage.*

**STOOPID**   Psst. God's hard drive crashed, eh? D'ya hear? It's
true.

*He makes smashing crashing sounds giggling and jumps to his
feet in a fake explosion, holds still cocky and cold like a coiled
snake, vicious and prone.*

God's hard drive crashed and all us little viruses spilled into
the streets. With a lust for blood. Spilled into the streets.
Started causing riots. We were at the heads of these angry
mobs, just wreaking havoc. Pretty soon buildings started
mysteriously catching fire all around the glittering fancy
town. Who'd have thought? First we took the Biggeddy wigs
and the Poodle ladies, all those rich selfish arrogant mother-
fuckers with the six figure incomes and the cars, houses, tax
loopholes and cellular phones to prove it died first. We set
them on fire. We did. The legislature towers and the ka*ching*
ka*ching* piggy bank cathedrals took a while what with them
being so heavily guarded, and the fancy town police
department loving to shoot at homeless people and punk
teenagers almost as much as they like killing Black kids. We

went crazy. Not crazy nuts. But crazy AAARGHGH. It was just the tip of the iceberg really. You should have seen what we did to the ratchetty inheritance horders. See, yuppie bureaucrats are one thing, but old money, now that really gets under my skin. Ya see, everybody always thought that the end of the world would come off the wing of some reckless third-world supersonic nuclear jet. *(He reverts to his plane mode and swoops down at the audience, making explosion sounds, and hurling more balloons.)* Everybody figured that the bombs would fall from the sky, but they didn't. They fell from our heads right into the pits of our stomachs and the intestinal mushroom cloud of apathy washed away everything, but that was just the beginning. It wuz the aftershock that got us. Rage. A huge ball of fiery rage that we just had to let out of our fingers and out through our hands. *(STOOPID draws one of his hands fast into a finger gun, a gunshot explodes through the sound system.)* Becuz, there's no more room inside. That's the real threat. The real killer. I'm a killer. I might look like a boy, but actually, I'm an explosive. My dick is a stick of dynamite, but some sonofabitch doctor cut off the fuse. *(He lights a cigarette.)* Still however the fact remains that I am right full of volatile substances. *(He blows smoke at the audience, FREAK and BUZZ slowly re-enter, crawling in.)* And when the smoke clears, we cannot allow ourselves to become our oppressor. We cannot allow ourselves to become the enemy. We cannot allow ourselves to turn into Old men. Men. I don't ever want to be a man. I don't ever wanna be a man.

FREAK     *(FREAK is prodding STOOPID, driving him.)* Son, you lazy bastard, what are you doing huh? What are you gonna do with yourself?—What are you gonna amount to? See. These are all questions that you have got to answer for yourself son—

STOOPID     Because for Chrissake son—at the rate you're going you'll end up—

FREAK &
STOOPID     *(jaggedly overlapping)* Goddamn it, boy—You'll never be anything—You'll be a loser—A goddamn loser—Jesus Christ—Don't talk back to me—You know what—Don't talk back to me—You'll be—Don't you fucking talk back to me—

Your mother and I, well hell your mother can't even look at ya without—Don't you tell me to fuck off—You fuck off—A burden to society—A useless worthless loser—Get the fuck—Don't you even—I don't ever want to see you again you little fuck. *(They punch out at nothing, rushing and grabbing each other.)*

STOOPID    Yeah men, right. A burden to society? Well, Daddy dearest, get with the program. I'm not a burden. I'm a cancer Daddy. An ugly little cancer devouring the earth. You sack of shit. Ha Ha. We're following the asphalt railways and the long shadows right across the universe Daddy, and we're burning down everything in our path. Ya see? And all this time you thought I'd wind up on welfare. Well, ya lack vision, Dad. Ya really do.

*Pause, seduction.*

FREAK    Oh, Stoopid, you are such an angry young man.

STOOPID    I'm a killer. I'm a stone cold killer.

FREAK    Nah. Nah. Yer a ferocious, young, virile killer.

STOOPID    Blood on my lips.

FREAK    Sweet blood. That sweet, sweet blood.

## Vicious Little Boyz in the Rain

*The lights shift to show RAIN, FREAK and STOOPID all asleep, curled up with each other like a pack of dogs. BUZZARD is standing down stage in front of them, adjusting his tie. He is now wearing the middle-aged man's suit which has huge gouges and bloodstains all over it. The lights are very low, and tender.*

**BUZZARD**     I've got a brother what lives in CaliNova. Ian. My momma sended him there when he got sick. She told me she sended him to this bewdiful place where he could play in the sun with all the other bewdiful kids, with fun rides and beaches and candy and see Freak says the place is CaliNova. And see my momma, she sended our family dog there, too. The dog, Santa, we got him for Christmas when we were really, well I wuz six and he wuz two-years, eight, so yeah, anyway she sended the dog down there so that Santa could be in the sun and play in the ocean. My momma, see, she figured that it would be best for him if he could do all that cuz he wuz really old and had bad legs, Santa not Ian, the dog. Ya know it's sad, Cuz when I wuz a teenager then Santa got old and fuck, that really fucked me up, cuz he wuz all crippled up when I wuz jus' well when I wuz not. I mean he wuz old, had mats and knots all over his chocolate coat, a chocolate lab. Such a bewdiful dog. He wuz so happy when he wuz a puppy. Ya know, when they have those huge feet and they're ears are always stickin' right up. He went blind in one eye. My momma told me it wuz cuz he had a "stroke." Bud I think it wuz cuz he wuz old. He limped. He would lay outside in our backyard and bugs would crawl all over him. I mean when I was a kid he wuz a kid, but then I just. I hate it. I'm not a dog, I know that. But I'm, it just it takes longer with people. D'ya get it? Whad I mean? Ya see. I don't want ever to be a man. I want always to be a little boy. And to have fun. Ya un-der-stand? See I'm goin' to CaliNova with Freak and I'm gunna see Santa. Good. Dog. *(He takes out a pair of binoculars and starts scanning the audience. He uses his hand as a gun and starts pegging off audience members while still looking through the binoculars. He catches something in his eye. Massive surge of light rising, he runs toward the audience adjusting his binoculars. Pause.)* Freak. Freak. Wake up. *(He goes to FREAK, crouches down and pulls at his jacket, FREAK stirs awake.)* Wake up. Freak, wake up. I kin. I kin see it. I kin see it.

## Vicious Little Boyz in the Rain

*Pale blue light on RAIN. RAIN puts out her hand and looks to the sky, it begins to lightly rain.*

**RAIN**  D'ya see me here? I'm beautiful, I'm quivering. D'ya see me? You're perfect. And you'll say, Oh yeah? And I'll say I'm just some kid who saw you in the rain in CaliNova and you'll say, no, no you're not, I'm not an ugly demon, no you're some beautiful kid in the rain in CaliNova. *(pause)* If I find you can we say that? can you say that? Can I hold you? Please. I found yer van. It was empty. But ya know, the blankets in the back were still all wet from our rainy little bodies. When it rains, in CaliNova, all you perfect beautiful things, all you butterflies must wash up out of the sand, don't cha? Do ya lay there, staring at the sky waiting for the sun to come back? That yellow twenty-four-hour sun. It's coming back again, I know it. I'm gonna walk through all the puddles till I see you. A perfect beautiful thing with blown glass muscles, that's you. And when I see you I'm gonna hold you, if you let me, until everything's all dry the wind's gonna blow the soft sand over top of both of us. And then we'll be CaliNova. Wendy, that rain'll wash everything away, all the blood even. And you'll giggle, but you won't have anything to be afraid of, becuz, becuz there won't be anything ferocious about me anymore, and there won't be any ugly demons. Just two little perfect beautiful things under the sand. You and me. You and me in sunny CaliNova. I'm sorry. *(pause)* I really miss you, Wendy. I really do. I don't care if you break me, and I don't care if I forget how to fly. I just want you. You and me in the sweet sand in Cali—Please just touch me, you? Please? *(BUZZ steps in from behind her and holds her tightly. Children's laughter. BUZZ and RAIN sadly waltz. Underscore with the whimpering dog.)*

## Vicious Little Boyz in the Rain

**RAIN**   Freak told me, see, I mean we all kinda agreed, right?
No Wendys allowed. No Wendys. No fucking. No fucking
Wendys. Cuz Boyz and Wendys are a "deadly combination."
Freak told me, see, that, fucking, it burns a little hole inta ya.
A place so hollow that ya can't do nothing ta fill it, see, and
once sumbuddy burns this hole inta ya, you'll never get it
back, never "you will never get complete revenge." Really.
See Freak told me, that the soft touches and the holds, and the
warm belly feelings are the ones that break yer bones the
hardest, ya shatter. And see fucking and falling in love makes
ya so brittle, and old. Fall in love ya get old. You get old you
die. You fall in love and you stay home, knitting by the fire-
place, and when Peter Pan comes crashing through that
window—you forget how to fly. Ya understand? Ya don't
want to be the loser who stays home in love and dies. No
Wendys. Cuz boyz and Wendys can make scary things inside
each other, things that'll break ya. Soft things. Crying things.
Things that ya hafta be be be scared of. Ugly things, and sad
trickles of blood in the sand, broken leaky hearts. *(A long
awkward pause. FREAK is pulling away from STOOPID.)* I'm
looking for any signs that we're in for trouble in there, right?
And it's raining, and I like the rain, that's why it's my name.
*(STOOPID gets up dusting himself off.)* I'm walking in the rain
and it's so easy, it keeps falling all night, and I'm staring at all
the lonely cars and eyeing all the passersby, and it's midnight,
and I'm feeling all dizzy, such soft easy rain, I walk through
puddles with sopping hair all coy and hungry trying not to
look suspicious, but the whole time I'm imagining I'm
beautiful with a beautiful walk and surrounded by butterflies
tired wet butterflies, and we're mumbling to each other, but
I mean, it's just silly boy nonsense, and I see this girl. *(FREAK
walks away down toward RAIN, watching her, his face turning
from curiosity to fury, he is witnessing the events of her story as she
tells them, STOOPID slowly follows, never taking his eyes off of
FREAK.)* And she's sitting on this curb, and I'm wishing
I could play with her hair.

## *Vicious Little Boyz in the Rain*

**FREAK**     *(complete narcotic state, rise explode)* With its twenty-four hour citrus sun *(He takes a grapefruit out of his satchel and holds it in the air above his head.)* miles of beaches. And there, there are silky bodied boys and girls with suckers in their mouths barefoot in the sand. And we can scream and swallow the ocean, and the saltwater will cascade through our veins and we'll be so pure. And we can run around on rollerskates past clowns on stilts. The merry-go-round with yer favourite horse. And you always get to it first. The tallest and whitest with that golden mane, green I love you eyes, and that tinkely tinkely sweet and free little song, *(He starts to spin.)* and she whirls and she spins and every time she rises you'd swear she would never come down. Never come down. Never ever come down. *(pause)* And, and. At night the stars just orbit the golden sun. Breathe. It's a beaUtiful world Stoopid. But you've got to keep your head up and your eyes in the sky with your hand holding the clouds, and stop digging up their ugly old dead from their ugly old dirt. *(He hurls the grapefruit at the ground and steps on it. He then stares at STOOPID. Picks up a chunk of the grapefruit, bites into it then spits the mouthful at STOOPID, there is something degrading and sexual about this act.)* Don't undermine the New. World. Order. With your guilty old soul. Now, stand up.

## *Boys* by Paul Dunn

PAUL DUNN began his playwrighitng career with *Boys*. He is also the author of *High-Gravel-Blind*, which opened the Studio Theatre at the Stratford Festival, and has been recorded as a radio drama for CBC. He has worked in theatres across the country as an actor, and is a graduate of the National Theatre School of Canada.

ℒ ℒ ℒ

### Synopsis

MIKE, JEFF and ANDY are all facing questions of identity. Who are they? How do they fit in? What do they want out of life? The three characters lean on varying crutches that give them a false sense of masculinity and purpose. For the three young men, the quest for their identities results in the realization of self.

MIKE is Ham-and-Cheese-Boy. Building sandwiches and jigsaw puzzles makes him feel macho, powerful and in control.

JEFF is Tambourine-Boy. His tambourine, (Satan), and the music of ABBA provide him with a fantasy of love and spirituality as well as a vent for his masculine passion and aggression.

The full script of *Boys* is available contained in the book, *Shakin' the Stage*, from Scirocco Drama, an imprint of J. Gordon Shillingford Publishing, www.jgshillingford.com.

## *Boys*

*MIKE at the sandwich factory, getting ready for work.*

**MIKE**    DO THINGS WELL AND WITH PASSION.

*He begins to work. Considerably less enthusiasm than before.*

Ham, cheese. Ham, cheese. Ham, cheese.

*A pause. A sigh. He's losing his rhythm.*

Ham.... Cheese, ham. Cheese. Ham cheese ham....
Cheeeeeeese. Arghhhh.

*A deep breath. And a violent attack—*

Ham cheese ham cheese ham cheese ham. Fuck. Fuck cheese
fuck me fuck THIS!

*Music cuts out sharply. The conveyor belt stops. He stares
down the audience.*

I may be on the front lines on the sandwich industry here,
and I may be the fucking commanding officer of the ham-
and-cheese squad, the one line of defence between that
Construction Worker and an empty lettuce-mustard bun
BUT—It's still a CRAPPY job making crappy sandwiches they
sell at corner stores and yeah, no matter how much I rock at
putting that ham on that cheese they're still GROSS.

Look around you, Ham-and-Cheese Boy. The other guys have
figured it out.

My lettuce girl could give a fuck. My Top-Bun-Boy just tossed
the buns on without even looking and I think my Mustard-
Boy is using his tongue.

They're looking at me like I'm a fool. Like they're asking
themselves—"Hey, that Ham-and-Cheese-Boy, he looks like
he really cares about that ham and cheese. Guess he hasn't
figured out his job's a joke, that it takes no skill—What is he,
a LOSER?" Yeah, Ham-and-Cheese-Boy, I think you might
just be a BIG FAT LOSER!

Yeah? YEAH? OH YEAH!?

Well I DON'T CARE ANYMORE!

I'm turning 22 in a week and this is my life? I'm not making a mark in this world.

*(big realization)* I'm not a God.... I hardly exist. What the fuck am I DOING HERE?!!!

WHAT ARE YOU LAUGHING AT LETTUCE-GIRL?

## *Boys*

**JEFF**   So the cops escort me into the station. Satan and I are in the grip of the enemy. Our only hope is to evoke the power of ABBA— *(He exclaims.)* ABBALICIOUSNESS!

*(quiet)* Name the song, Satan. Name the song.

> *SATAN speaks in tambourine.*

Of course.

> *"Dancing Queen" plays—a disco ball, ABBAlicious lighting. He is filled with the spirit of ABBA.*

Beauty, grace and power flow from us. Everyone in the station is drawn into our spell. The cops stand in awe, handcuffed drug pushers sway to the rhythm, the woman answering the phones puts everyone on hold, smiles big and even hums along. I inch towards the door, ready to make my escape. No one can resist the power of the dancing.... WHAT!?

They've called my "mom" and I can hear her crying on the other end—

No, don't pass the phone to me, yes, I know she's crying but she's not my real—FINE, I'll talk to her—

> *The disco ball and music end abruptly. On the phone:*

Yes. I lied. I hit the old man because he was trying to take my spot and the other guy—No. I'm not on drugs, Mom, please, I had to lie because you—no, I'm not blaming you, yes, I'm an adult now, no no no no no no no what if I don't come home, Mom? What if I don't come home ever again? GOODBYE!

She's fine.

So... you gonna cuff me or what? Oh. A "warning." *(a wink to the audience)* Uh... thanks.

> *Again to the audience, nodding knowingly.*

Abbalicious.

## *Martian Summer* by Nathalie Boisvert
## translated by Bobby Theodore

NATHALIE BOISVERT's first work, *L'histoire sordide de Conrad B*, was at the Festival international de Spa 1997, in Belgium. and then, a second time in Brussels where it won a prize. She wrote *L'été des Martiens*, simultaneously produced at Théâtre Périscope in Québec city and in Montauban, France. The play was also produced in Belgium, in Charleroi and at le Théâtre de Poche de Bruxelles in 2000. The English translation of the play, by Bobby Theodore, was produced in 2002 by Theatre Direct Canada at Theatre Passe Muraille in Toronto, and has also been translated in to German by Frank Heibert. It was produced at the Landestheatre and the Grips in Germany in March 2006.

BOBBY THEODORE lives in Montréal and is a graduate of the National Theatre School of Canada's playwriting program. His first translation was produced across Canada and earned him a nomination for the Governor General's Award for Literary Translation in 2000. Since then, he has gone on to translate more than 12 plays.

ꙅ    ꙅ    ꙅ

**Synopsis**

PEANUT and KIKO are teenage loners leading painful and desolate lives. One summer KIKO reveals to PEANUT her plans to rendezvous with an alien spacecraft, convincing PEANUT to do the same. *"When does childhood end? Is there a line drawn on the ground, that I can jump over without being caught?"* *Martian Summer* is a crusade from the dusk of childhood to the dawn of adulthood. For KIKO the rite of passage is littered with danger and fear, for PEANUT the stakes are much higher. *Martian Summer* is a rare Quebecois translation commissioned by an English language theatre company.

Note: *Martian Summer* was originally written to be performed by boys, the gender of the characters was switched for the Theatre Direct production.

The full script of *Martian Summer* is available from Theatre Direct.

## Martian Summer

**PEANUT**   It's over, Kiko. We're screwed.

**KIKO**   Peanut! Stop it! You'll see, it'll be fine. Hey, imagine, if we make it to another galaxy... we'll be able to do anything. Bringing back the dead... that's nothing. Technology, Peanut, don't forget technology, they know way more than we do.

**PEANUT**   It's over.

**KIKO**   Peanut! Peanut, you hear that?

**PEANUT**   It's the police. They're coming to get us.

**KIKO**   No, no, not that... in the sky.

**PEANUT**   What's that! Looks like a helicopter...

**KIKO**   It's not a helicopter. It's them. They're coming. We're going to leave soon.

**PEANUT**   It's a helicopter. In five minutes, our lives will be over. We're going to end up in a grey, concrete cell and rot for the rest of our lives.

**KIKO**   (taking PEANUT by the shoulders) You're wrong Peanut. It's them. We're going! We're gone! We'll never go to school again. You'll never have to play dodge-ball again. Big Julie will stay down here, with the worms, while we float like soap bubbles on some planet where the atmosphere will be so light that we won't feel a thing anymore. We won't feel anything, Peanut! We'll laugh like crazy! We won't think about here anymore. You'll be able to talk to Sylvie and she'll answer. She'll finally be able to answer you.

**PEANUT**   The police are getting closer. I hear them.

**KIKO**   You'll be able to chuck your glasses in the garbage. They'll make your eyes better and you'll see better than anybody else. There won't be any more fucking TV so someone, I mean, the aliens will invent new games for us, and they'll show us how to fly spaceships. We'll be able to fly all over the whole universe. We won't need anybody anymore. We won't need money anymore.

**PEANUT**   It's a helicopter, Kiko...

**KIKO**   You can't see! It's them. They'll find us alien parents. We'll live in hanging houses with glass walls that we can walk through like ghosts. We won't have to ask for permission to do what we want anymore. We won't have to work when we grow up, we won't have to eat, or sleep or put up with people we hate.

**PEANUT**   Stop it, Kiko!

**KIKO**   Look up there. What do you see?

**PEANUT**   A helicopter.

**KIKO**   You're wrong. A helicopter is bigger and makes more noise. It doesn't shine like that and it's not as round.

**PEANUT**   Are you sure?

**KIKO**   Peanut, I have good eyes. Trust me, it's them. We're going to make it, Peanut. We're going to make it. I swear...

**PEANUT**   If they come.

**KIKO**   It's them. They're coming.

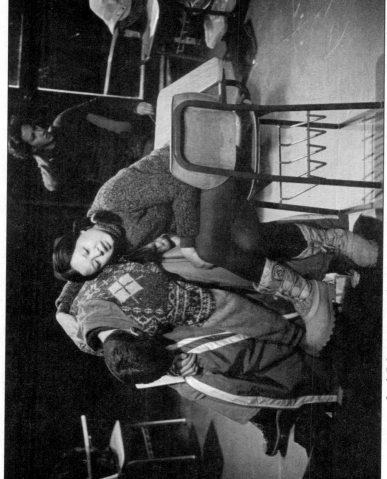

Jacob Baker, Marjorie Chan and Michelle Polak in *Roundabout*, 2002.

*photo by Andrew Oxenham*

## *Roundabout* by Sean Reycraft

*See Sean Reycraft's biography on page 64.*

൮  ൮  ൮

### Synopsis

*"You don't hear anything—not nothing for the longest time, but then your heart starts. It's in your head but then your heart starts. It's in your head like it's knocking soft at first but then SLAM as it tries to get out. So it becomes a game—nothing but a game."* Trapped in a classroom on a snow day, GORDIE, MOLLY and KRISTY go round and round in a dark comedy exploring the issues of peer pressure and power in relationships. Innocent games morph into schemes of entrapment, isolation and conformity in *Roundabout* when the present crashes with the past to reveal a haunting history.

The full script of *Roundabout* is available through Playwrights Guild of Canada, www.playwrightsguild.ca.

## Roundabout

**KRISTIE**    And "everybody" is a blame of brilliance? I hate love. It really pisses me off. Usually I like it. Usually it's pretty great. Like when you're at a dance and you're really bored? Or when you wanna call somebody other than a girl. Or when you feel like staring dreamy into somebody's eyes— and that feeling as they stare all dreamy into yours. But then it changes—becomes something else. And then it's more scary than a screaming French teacher. More stupid than spending all day stuck here. And more fragile than—than nine thousand eggs driving through a snowstorm. So I'm not gonna blame you—I'm not gonna blame anybody. I'm gonna blame love 'cause it changed you don't have any—for me anymore.

> *Beat.*

And you used to.

> *KRISTIE stands and pushes her desk to the side of the class.*

**MOLLY**    I'm sorry, Kristie. I'm sorry but I think you win.

> *GORDIE turns away from KRISTIE. Seeing this, KRISTIE pulls on her coat and hat.*

**KRISTIE**    I'm gonna go. So I'm gonna call my grandma—she'll drive over and get me. She's not supposed to drive—least not in weather like this, but if I ask her she'll come. She'll drive over. She'll get me so you don't have to worry. You don't have to care. I'll be fine.

> *KRISTIE leaves.*

> *Long pause.*

**GORDIE**    I love you.

> *GORDIE stands.*

I should go after her.

> *GORDIE sits.*

That was—I like you. No—"you look pretty good from a long ways away." Like if I saw you down a street I'd wanna keep walking—or I'd wanna cross over if you were on the other side. And I wouldn't get pissed off. I wouldn't be disappointed which I guess means you look pretty good close up. *(standing)* I should really go see how she's doing. *(sitting)* I wanna be here. I wanna stay here and try to figure out why even though I've known you since grade one when we were—what? Five? Six? And I guess kids who are five or six don't think about things like dating or kissing or having— *(standing)* and I should really go see if she's okay. *(sitting)* But last summer your dad hired me to be a lifeguard—head lifeguard, like it's important—and it was a good job sitting, watching—that got me money—not big money, but money to buy a Coke and a bag of Crunchits everyday from you. And we got into this thing you and me—this kinda "thing" where you'd be mean and not look at me or talk to me 'cept to say "fuck off" when I tried to buy smokes. I started to like it. I started to like you.

> *GORDIE stands—then sits again.*

And I didn't know Simon would take it serious. I was just having him over—having him around. Trying to figure out how I could get you to be mean to me on a new improved boyfriend-and-girlfriend level. That's it. That's all. But I'm sorry. I'm really sorry. I been wanting to tell you that for a few months—okay, six—but it's taken me this long to—

> *GORDIE stands, then sits, then stands again.*

See, it's not a stupid love. It's not a "hope we get the same classes and she lets me sit with her at lunch" love. It's a "I feel fucked up and shitty and I bet she does too" love. I bet she understands. I bet you know. Which is where I started when I told you "I love you."

**MOLLY**   Right.

**GORDIE**   I do—I love you.

**MOLLY**   We're at a party.

**GORDIE**    What?

**MOLLY**   Pretend we're at a party. A Christmas party—no, a birthday party. No—one of those "my parents are in Mexico and I'm having a rockin' party" party? Or no. A pool party.

**GORDIE**    What?

**MOLLY**    We're at a pool party. And I got dragged along, acting all "I'd rather be elsewhere" but I don't. I don't. 'Cause inside there's punch. Inside there's chips. Inside there's pop music on a clock radio that's playin' real loud. And inside—inside there's you. There's also eight or nine other lifeguards, but most important there's you. And about ten minutes into it I pull you outside where nobody is 'cause it's raining and for the first time, I—

*MOLLY stands, readies herself.*

Stay there.

**GORDIE**    Okay.

**MOLLY**    Put your arms at your sides.

## *Misha* by Adam Pettle

ADAM PETTLE was born and raised in Toronto. His first play, *Therac 25* (Scirocco Drama, 2000), has received numerous productions across the country and has been adapted for CBC Radio. His play *Zadie's Shoes* (Scirocco, 2001) premiered at Factory Theatre in 2001 and was subsequently picked up by Mirvish Productions and ran at the Wintergarden Theatre beginning in March 2002. His most recent play is *Sunday Father* (Scirocco, 2003). Adam is currently the playwright-in-residence at the Canadian Stage Company.

ᔑ  ᔑ  ᔑ

### Synopsis

*"Do you know what the word for kiss in Hebrew is? Nesheck. Do you know what the word for gun is? Nesheka. Same word. Funny that."* *Misha* deconstructs the account of a violent schoolyard murder where one young Jew kills a fellow Jew. MAX, the survivor, is drowning himself in Seconal and Vodka, courting his own thoughts of suicide, and running from the truth. Determined not to be silenced, the voices of violence, guilt, betrayal, friendship, and faith are exposed.

The full script of *Misha* is available contained in the book, *Shakin' the Stage*, from Scirocco Drama, an imprint of J. Gordon Shillingford Publishing, www.jgshillingford.com.

## *Misha*

**MAX**     Fact. My parents would give me a second circumcision if they ever caught me reading the New Testament.

Ms. McTierney gave me this *(holding up the bible)* at Mish's funeral. She told me to, "Look to it now for all the answers." Now if only I knew the fucking questions. I always told Mish that she was a Bible thumper. I mean you can tell by the way she taught World Issues. All the real problems in the world always seemed to be happening in the countries that aren't Christian. That and she always wears these pin-striped button-downs, buttoned all the way to the top... a sure sign that no one but Jesus was ever going to get in there. I was going to throw it away but then I didn't know the protocol... I mean if breaking a mirror is seven years bad luck what do you get for chucking a Bible? So, I kept it and I have to say it has come in handy, a little late-night/early-morning reading. Fact. I don't sleep anymore. I don't sleep because of my dreams. I dream—

## *Misha*

MISHA   So, this guy Max he only learned half of the lines
right? His half of the lines. Makes sense, don't do anymore
work than you have to. So, the time comes and he's standing
up there ready to go, ready to close the deal. But before he
can get out his first line, the congregation starts in, they sing
the opening line, they sing his line. So now he's totally fucked
because he doesn't know the next line or any of his lines for
that matter and he can't read Hebrew and he's... what's he
going to do? It's the tribe right and they're all sitting there
staring at him and he's... he's got to respond something. So,
he croaks out a few Hebrew sounds, a *cha* and he throws in
a *melech*... but he's fucking dying up there. And no one...
here's the part that I can't... no one jumps in to help him.
I mean anyone out there knows Hebrew knows he's dying.
Anyone out there knows that he's lost and reaching and that
he needs help... but they don't... they just let him stand up
there. Sixteen bars of dying... fucking song lasted a week
I bet. Why wouldn't they do anything? Sing his lines with
him. Laugh at it all with him. Make him feel like this song,
this service has nothing to do with anything and that he will
still become a good man if he does good things. Why didn't
they do anything, Cohen?

*Beat.*

## *Misha*

**MAX**  And so I can't move forward. Only back... to the beginning.

*He takes a fifth Seconal.*

He came here in the fifth grade. Lived in the "jungle." That big apartment building on the other side of Fenster, that's what every one calls it. And because he lived on that side of Fenster he should've gone to Stanton Park but somehow... I never asked him why but some how he ended up at Glenvale. In Mrs. Downey's split four/five class. And for the first two months of that year no one heard him say anything, not a word. All we knew about him was that he was from Russia and so we started calling him "Silent Sergei."

And then one day... it was like November and I was sitting in the lunch room and my best friend Alex McLean was home faking sick, so I was kind of bored. And I looked over to where Mish was sitting at this big table all alone as per usual. And I... now I am *not* the kind of guy that would usually go over and make nice with the pasty foreigner but for some reason... you know how sometimes when you see someone eating alone it can give you the saddest feeling in the world...? Especially if what they're eating is like soup or chili or something. Well, he was spooning borscht out of this see-through Tupperware thing and he had some... some borscht on his chin and for some reason I couldn't... and so I... I went over to him, sat down beside him and said "Hi, I'm Max Cohen." And he looked up at me, beets shmeared all over his... he gave me this huge smile and said—

## *The Phoenix Rides a Skateboard* by Kate Rigg

KATE RIGG was born in Toronto to an Indonesian mother and an Australian father. She is the writer of cult hits *Kate's Chink-0-Rama: Featuring the Chink-0-Rama Dancers* and *Birth of an ASIAN*. She is known for irreverent stand-up comedy and has spoken on/written about race and representation in *Time* magazine, *The Globe and Mail*, *The San Francisco Examiner*, *NPR-Pacific Time*, *THIS* magazine, *NOW* magazine and *A* magazine.

ဢ ဢ ဢ

**Synopsis**

KIM is a young CanAsian adoptee searching the internet for clues to her past and direction for her future. After entering the terraneous world of skate culture she connects to the board beneath her feet and KIM/Betty P cruises forward toward her own rad-style. In crafting this vision-quest, Rigg kick-flips Asian stereotypes and confronts cultural identity politics.

The full script of *The Phoenix Rides a Skateboard* is available contained in the book, *Shakin' the Stage*, from Scirocco Drama, an imprint of J. Gordon Shillingford Publishing, www.jgshillingford.com.

## *The Phoenix Rides a Skateboard*

*BARB, a friendly neighbourhood organizer, has a clipboard and wears a sun visor with a Canada Goose on it.*

**BARB**   Well, crikey on a bikey I for one am as glad as Sinbad to have a little addition to our block. Thanks heavens for little Kim, eh? Finally a lucky break for John and Mary. They were positively obsessed you know... talked about nothing else at our joint garage sales for the last three years, and now, they have a new slant on life! Oh, whoops, sorry oopsy daisy!

OK. So anyhoo, I thought it would be very neighbourly for us to all get together you know as a community for this assimilation sensitivity seminar? Twinkie anyone? Banana bread?

OK so as I was saying let's make sure the Whitebreads feel our support, OK? Now Janis, you and Gordie are in charge of the fundraising garage sales so's we can start that college mutual fund. You know those Asian kids just root and toot in the math and sciences so we can all get that little MD on her way, eh? OK an oriental theme is what Marjorie proposed I think that's a very good idea, oh sorry, right, Pan-Asian theme. A kind of dragon-y paper lantern-y feel. I have some left over lichees from our Hawaiian night so we could do a lichee lemonade stand for the kids, you get the idea, just make it festive and exotic like Market Street.

OK so now for the sensitivity part. Please refer to the pamphlets I have created of fun facts and easy-to-follow tips about how to make foreigners feel more welcome.

OK number one. Don't stare. That means you, Phyllis, you'll stare at a recycling bin if it's new on the block. So watch it, foreigners always know if you're staring. Number two, try to refrain from talking about sweatshops, underage prostitution, malnutrition, sedition, SARS, religious persecution, falun gong, foot-binding, Suzy Wong, Charlie Chan, ancient Chinese secrets, opium, ping-pong, burlesque, leprosy, abject poverty, public executions and stone throwing around our integrated family, it sends the wrong message, OK? No but yes.

Now there's some nice recipes in the back for rice casseroles and noodle pies in case you have them over for dinner and a list of suitable topics for conversation such as flower arrangement, Japanimation, rock gardens and Connie Chung's impact on broadcast journalism pre- and post Maury Povich. Above all, act normal. We don't want the little nipper to feel like a freak.

## The Phoenix Rides a Skateboard

*She's bright, popular and precocious. She wears a sweater set and looks at her nails a whole lot.*

**JOSSIE**     Yeah so Kim went to some other school up till grade 7 and 8 and we all thought she'd be good at algebra and stuff but actually she sucks at all science classes. I personally think she's fronting just to be cool coz everyone knows Asians are the best at math. But actually, you know, Kim is kind of different anyways, you know when she first got here no one really "got her." She was all quiet at first and we thought she might be an ESL student in the wrong class or some fresh-off-the-boat refugee case coz she was all quiet you know like a lot of them. I think it's upbringing or tradition, except her clothes were too cool, I mean not weird like old 80s crap or Salvation Army stuff like what they give to immigrants for free, or whatever. But yeah. Then I guess she started to get more comfortable because by grade ten she was just hanging out in the halls and on lunch like everyone else and we even invited her to go for dim sum with us on the weekend coz you know why not? And she's like, OK, and then stupid Dorie goes, "Are you an expert on dumplings?" and I am like "duhhh-hh… earth to nimrod… Kim is not even like the other ones Dorie! She's not even really Asian she's just Canadian like you and me—do you think she's some stupid ching chong ning nong pang pang pang ping pong pow?" like "me so horney/numba 14 deep fried wonton?"

And I can see Kim out of the corner of my eye she looks like she's about to cry right, because it is very important that your friends get who you are you know?

And Dorie just like must have made her feel I dunno stupid or something or weird so I go to Dorie:

"Are you demented? Do you think Kim is like some chink walking down Dundas with an upside down roast duck in her pocket and a coolie hat? Or some cleaning lady who no speaka de English? Or like that crazy lady with one tooth who tap dances outside the Eaton Centre in that weird dress? Or like some Japanese tourist taking pictures of the CN Tower going AH SO Big Tower-ah!?" "Hello!" I said, "Earth to dorkie this is your friend, hi this is Kim? Remember? What are you trying to do make her feel like some freak?"

Some people are so insensitive. Right? So we took her for some dim sum to make her feel better.

## *The Phoenix Rides a Skateboard*

*Skater music in.*

**KIM**   This is how I knew I would be a skater chick one day.

At the end of sixth grade I dream.

I'm on a skateboard in Chinatown.

I'm skating on streetcar tracks like a monorail from Disney.

Everything around me is twirling like dolls in a Christmas window.

*Delivery turns slam-poet style, accelerating as the images come.*

Old man

shopkeeper

face like a wrinkled frog

Tall kid in baggy pants

Spiky hair, neon beeper

Pokemons on hooded Ts

Stop-watches, wind-up dolls

Turtles, fish

Peanut stalls

In my face, a human race

Rushing feet, plastic bags

Bitter taste, chili paste

Sweet and sour spice racks

Perfume shops, fried pork chops

Girls in Hello Kitty shirts

Sunglasses, lemongrasses

Girls with Hello Kitty skirts

Roast pork bun, steamed dim sum

Waiters rushing past with carts

Skinny guys, slanty eyes

Smoking joints from their smoking hearts

Torn apart

Calendars with pretty girls, silk smocks, stores piled high

Powders, roots, dried up skins, bits of rock,

I can't stop...

Chinatown

the smell of blood, the smell of rain gushing down

Chinatown

in my face a human race

From alleys, small doorways waves of eyes rushing by

What do they see? Do they recognize?

Almond eyes and black hair, skin like an amber locket

I'm afraid of my own skin closing in

I reach into my blue jeans pocket

Pull out my school ID, see?

"This is me!"

I call out but there's no sound.

Chinatown

The smell of blood, the smell of rain

As my skin closes in again

Right next to my cheek a sea of freaks

Breathing in, breathing out

Frantically I try to speed up

I lack the skills, my wheels lock

They just spin on the ground, grinding sounds

Then someone else begins to sing

A chicken man or a witch doctor

And a million hands touching me

I don't know if I should laugh or cry.

I hear my name spoken over and over again

Spoken as if from some sacred place

Where prayers come from and incense is burned

I don't know where to turn

Or if I should...

My wheels lock, my throat still blocked

I am caught, suspended.

And I ask myself

How did I get here?

How did I get here?

My wheels finally unlock with a jolt

And suddenly I'm flying.

Suddenly everything is easy

Again

And I might be doing the most rad tricks on the best board

And Chinatown

Still below

I feel my blood rushing, I feel the rain gushing

I am flying now on a board

And I never need to touch sidewalk,

Again.

## The Phoenix Rides a Skateboard

*This one is a tech geek.*

**SKATER DUDE**    OK OK OK. So OK, look. First of all OK, here at Blades, OK we don't just sell the things, you know? We live the stuff! We get it right into the centre of our big bad um you know, bean enchilada or whatever, so let's get something straight here, girlie. If yer gonna be a chick who skates, OK then you're called a Skate Betty now, and you need to wear that title with pride. I mean we are serious about skating in this place and if you ever want to live skatelife or just come where skaters are and get help with your board or your technique the whole fish-taco of it, you have to respect your inner skater, you know? You have to respect the road to the skater way, you know? I mean the equipment the clothes the music, the tricks, the meets, the art the language, the history, the sponsors, the stars, the injuries, the risk, the exhilaration of the whole mondo experience. No one gives a shizznit about how many tricks you can do or how high you can ollie, if you are in skatelife, if you have respect for those who do it like breathing, then you can make up your own style your own rules and your own title. The rules are there are no rules, hehehe. Just like every board is different, and feels different, you are the rad creator of your own mad vibe. You just have to do it, though, own it for real, coz no one can do it for you, no one can show you your own rad style, you follow? OK get some pads and get out there and learn to ollie. Hehe. Betty.

## *The Phoenix Rides a Skateboard*

*JOSSIE is a little older and a little quicker now, and little more up on herself. She wears the same sweater set as before, with some indoor-clear shades pulled down low on her nose, which she also uses to point and gesture with.*

**JOSSIE**     OK so I tell right I say, to Kimmmmm, first of all, I don't see why you gotta act so weird now all the time all of a sudden anyways Kimmmmm. Right? Don't you even know that Betty is a loser term that dumb skate dorks use to patriarchally oppress girls in extreme sports, uh DUH! Yaaah! Hello! And I told her, right, um, do not be complicit in this um, ok radical dispossession of women by saying you're a Betty.

Because you remember when I stood up for her when like Dorie was all misguided about her being a chink in the multicultural mosaic of Grade Nine, but ummm we're in grade eleven now, this is the post Mariah Carey generation, and it's time for us to take a personal inventory of our female-ness our womanocity. Not only is it just weird for her to be in those Linkin Park T-shirts—all fronting like she's hard and everything, wearing millions of hard bracelets and all, I mean does she even know what a turn off to guys that is? And I can't be all hanging out with someone who threatens the natural order of our cafeteria.

So someone else better talk to her soon and it can't be me coz I am THIS close to being nominated for school spirit this year and I don't need anyone thinking I'm weird or dispossessed by association.

## *The Phoenix Rides a Skateboard*

*A white guy who wishes he was a little cooler than he is. He is better looking than the other two and more hyper.*

**SKATER DUDE**     Well alright then! Yeah! Yeah! The ollie! Yeah the basic trick! Look I can describe it to ya but when you git down to it, I mean you can't teach the ollie. Girl! It's a pop of the tail off hard cement, back foot, back foot, back foot… jumps! As you slide your front foot along the smooth deck and the board just goes pop! And then evens out in the air and and anddddd, you drop. But the descriptionation don't mean nothing until you try the machination of the ollie's flyeration for yourself. And if you can ollie, if you can ollie yeah! You have the basis for every trick every flip trick and grind and twist there is. You can ollie up a curb down some stairs onto a rail, wherever. It can take years to perfect the ollie coz you know you can always jump higher, cleaner, more perfect. The record is like 4 feet something. Man, Tony Hawk can ollie like a dream onto any surface, over obstacle courses, over a car! Your ollie will rocket at first, I mean for sure. Especially since you are a girl, no offence. Rocket is when the board barely leaves the ground and kinda points up in the air like a rocket. You got to clean that shit up before you even attempt your first flip. Get one of the dudes sitting outside to show you their moves after you pay for all the gear. Yah girl! Go git it! Skateration in the skater nation! Yeah!

## *The Phoenix Rides a Skateboard*

*Some web cam used on KIM here.*

**KIM**    So I'm freaking out in this dream.

I'm sitting on the ground.

I must be five years old or something.

Unable to move. I'm freaking.

In front of me Mom and Dad are waving at me from a big white roller coaster all covered in red maple leafs. They shout and wave like little kids and I keep reaching out my hand to them as they swoosh past me at a million miles per hour. Behind me a chicken van with two old chicken men selling fried chicken. They throw the bones at me and I pick them up off the ground looking for some meat.

Mom and Dad are laughing and laughing and waving as they spin and dip on the Maple Leaf and the little chicken men are laughing and laughing as they throw and pitch greasy naked bones at me. And I am hungry and everyone is laughing at me and I don't know how to talk now I am just a little kid so I just open my mouth and holler for help. Like heeeeeellllllllll-lllllp.

Everything feezes.

Roller coaster stops mid hill and starts moving all slowly backwards. Mom and Dad still waving and laughing but it's all backwards. And the chicken men close up the van and move away backing up backwards. And I don't know where to look I try to jump but my legs are so weak and I am caught, suspended unable to get anywhere fast, I hear the chicken men start to call me from inside the truck and Mom and Dad are calling me begging me to join them up there and I feel like I'm going to explode in all directions and I am never going to be safe or feel at home anywhere stuck in between the sound of everyone laughing backwards in slow motion and all I can say is

Heeeeeeeelllllllllllp.

I wake up. I'm in my room and I have no idea how I got here. Help? Help?

*Bleary-eyed, she gets up and attempts an ollie with her board. It sucks. Tries again. It sucks again.*

## *Not Quite the Same* by Anne Chislett

ANNE CHISLETT's plays have been produced across Canada and in the United States. *The Tomorrow Box* became a hit in Japan where it has toured to more than a hundred cities and has been produced three times in Tokyo. The Japanese translation by Toyoshi Yoshihara has recently been published in hardcover. Chislett's *Quiet in the Land* won the Governor-General's Award for Drama and the Chalmers Canadian Play Award (1983). *Flippin' In* won the Chalmers Canadian Play Award in the Theatre for Young Audiences division (1996). *Not Quite the Same* was nominated for both the Dora Mavor Moore and Chalmers awards. Other plays include *Yankee Notions* and *Another Season's Promise* (written with Keith Roulston). She was Artistic Director of the Blyth Festival, a unique summer theatre producing new Canadian plays, (which she co-founded), from 1998 to 2002.

∽ ∽ ∽

### Synopsis

*Not Quite the Same* follows a young girl named KYRA from the day of her birth, when her fairy godmother blesses her with an abundance of musical talent, up to her early adolescence. KYRA is caught in the struggle to reconcile her gift of music with her desire for a "normal and happy life."

The full script of *Not Quite the Same* is available from Playwrights Guild of Canada, www.playwrightsguild.ca.

## *Not Quite the Same*

**MAYLYNN**  "Kyra Hoffman played the piano last evening as many a full-grown musician couldn't if they tried."

**KYRA**  "A genius she is, with the modesty that only true genius knows."

**MAYLYNN**  "Every detail of her playing…"

**KYRA**  "A fearless authority and finesse we have not heard since the debut of Glenn Gould."

**MAYLYNN**  I guess that's good, eh?

**KYRA**  It's good, it's fantastic, it's totally awesome.

**MAYLYNN**  So who is Glenn Gould?

**KYRA**  Just Canada's most famous piano player ever! I've got all his CDs. Want to hear one?

**MAYLYNN**  What I meant was…. What was he like?

**KYRA**  I don't know, but his music is really amazing.

**MAYLYNN**  *(looking at the CD cover)* He looks kinda cute. At least— *(shuffling through CDs)* before he got old. He looks really strange in this one.

**KYRA**  Yeah… I guess he sort of does.

**MAYLYNN**  So—was he as strange as he looks?

**KYRA**  The liner notes don't say much about his life…

**MAYLYNN**  Well if you're going to be like him, don't you think we should do a little investigating?

**KYRA**  Mom, are there any books about Glenn Gould?

**MOM**  I think we have one—here. Your father tried to read it, but he said it was too boring. …Here it is.

**KYRA**  *The Ecstasy and Tragedy of Genius.*

**MAYLYNN**  Tragedy? Whoa, Kyra, this doesn't sound good.

**KYRA**  *(reading)* Hmmm.

**MAYLYNN**   Look there's a whole bunch of pictures! Did he date any movie stars?

**KYRA**   Movie stars?

**MAYLYNN**   Oh, there aren't any pictures of him at parties or anything! He's always by himself.

**KYRA**   Here's one with his dog.

**MAYLYNN**   Yeah, but… did he ever get married? Did he have kids?

**KYRA**   I don't think so…

**MAYLYNN**   Glenn Gould: A Solitary Figure. It sure doesn't sound like it. Oh, that's so sad.

**KYRA**   I guess.

**MAYLYNN**   I don't think I'd like to live alone all the time. I want to get married some day, don't you?

**KYRA**   *(reading)* Hmmm.

**MAYLYNN**   So… of all the boys at school, who do you think about? I know who thinks about you.

**KYRA**   Who?

**MAYLYNN**   DEREK!

**KYRA**   Derek?

**MAYLYNN**   So… you like him?

**KYRA**   He's okay.

**MAYLYNN**   At least he's not bad looking…

**KYRA**   Not bad… he's gorgeous!

**MAYLYNN**   Hey, I'll bet Derek'll be at the grade eight dance next week…. Let's go.

**KYRA**   I don't think so.

**MAYLYNN**   Why not?

**KYRA**   I'd just end up standing around all night. I mean, nobody ever talks to me… except you.

**MAYLYNN**   Yeah, but you don't talk to them either. Like—all they see is a girl standing by herself with eyes glazed over humming Mozart or something. I mean, Kyra, you can't blame anybody for thinking you're kinda...

**KYRA**   Kinda what?

**MAYLYNN**   Well... you know... different.

**KYRA**   You mean weird, don't you?

**MAYLYNN**   No. Listen, Kyra, remember that day we played ball? Lots of kids wanted to be your friend? You even got invited to a couple parties.

**KYRA**   It was right before my concert. I didn't have time to go anywhere.

**MAYLYNN**   You could have made the volleyball team if you tried.

**KYRA**   I can't do sports, Maylynn. I might...

**MAYLYNN**   Hurt your hands, I know.

**KYRA**   I guess people think that's kind of dumb.

**MAYLYNN**   I think it's dumb that you never get to have any fun at all. *(KYRA doesn't respond.)* Look, the concert's over now. You can take a break from practising for one night, can't you?

**KYRA**   Maybe...

**MAYLYNN**   So, you'll come to the dance? Please, Kyra. I don't want to go alone. Come for my sake?

**MOM**   *(off)* Kyra.... It's time for Maylynn to go now.

**MAYLYNN**   Please, Kyra.

**KYRA**   I'll think about it, okay?

**MAYLYNN**   Okay.

## *Trickster Tale* by Tomson Highway

TOMSON HIGHWAY is one of Canada's leading playwrights, as well as an author of fiction and a musician. He has written eight plays, including *The Rez Sisters* (1988), which won a Dora Mavor Moore Award and *Dry Lips Oughta Move to Kapuskasing* (1989), which received both a Dora Mavor Moore Award and a Chalmers Award. Mr. Highway's first novel, *Kiss of the Fur Queen* (Doubleday) appeared in 1998, and his first children's book, *Caribou Song*, which is bilingual in Cree and English, was released in fall 2002.

∽ ∽ ∽

### Synopsis

Called Weesageechak by the Cree, Nanabush by the Ojibway, Iktomi by the Sioux, Raven on the West Coast, Glooscap in the east, Coyote on the Plains, this Trickster goes by many names and guises. In fact, transformer that he is, he can take on any shape that he chooses, in the case of this particular show, a sort of half-man (or woman) and half-spider, which is how the Sioux of North and South Dakota conceive of IKTOMI, their version of the Trickster.

...In the show, IKTOMI, the Sioux Spiderman, goes out into the world and, like Dorothy in "The Wizard of Oz," meets up with several characters along the way, one after another after another, in this case in twos and threes. He gets hopelessly entangled in their lives only to find out, in the end, that much as he would like to "use" them to his own advantage, THEY are the ones who end up with the last laugh.

—Tomson Highway

The full script of *Tickster Tale* is available from Theatre Direct.

## *Trickster Tale*

**IKTOMI**    How many restaurants do you think there are in this town, this city, in the province, the country, the world? Can you count them? Why, on every block, are there not two, three, four, five, maybe six, maybe ten? Twenty? In this city alone, are there not maybe, what? Fifty thousand restaurants? Sixty thousand? Half a million? Why so many, you may ask? And are they all necessary?

> *Mass-mastication starts playing softly on sound system, getting louder and louder and louder, until the whole world seems to be masticating, a disturbing, surrealistic effect.*

And everywhere you go, are there not men and women just biting and chewing and swallowing and biting and chewing and swallowing and chomping and gnawing and devouring and chomping and gnawing and devouring and drooling, masticating, drooling, masticating? Look around you as you walk down the street. That's all they're doing is eating, are they not? And what are they eating, you may ask? Flesh, might you say? Flesh of what? Or of whom? Flesh of cow, of pig, of chicken, of sheep, lamb, goose, duck, moose, caribou, goat, trout, shark, cod, pickerel and flesh of carrot, of potato, of onion, of broccoli—I mean, now I ask you, my dears, are these not living, breathing beings just as well as humans? Are these not living, breathing, sensate creatures just like you, you, you, you? And *moi*?

> *By this time, the rabbit, looking disturbingly human, lies astride IKTOMI's plate, IKTOMI sitting at table with knife and fork poised for the onslaught.*

So why are you staring at me like that? As if you, in your life, have never ever seen such a thing as a creature about to sink his teeth into the flesh of another friendly, fellow creature and then biting and chewing and swallowing and chomping and gnawing and devouring? Do you not do it, too? And where, pray tell me, would you be if you didn't?

## *Alphonse* by Wajdi Mouawad
### translated by Shelley Tepperman

WAJDI MOUAWAD is Lebanese in his childhood, French in his way of thinking and Québécois in his theatre. Since graduating from the National Theatre School of Canada, Wajdi Mouawad has written, adapted, translated and directed stage plays for audiences of all ages. *Littoral* (*Tideline*) won a Governor General's Award for Drama in 2000 and Wajdi was nominated for this award again for his play *Rêves* (*Dreams*). From 2000–2004, he was at the helm of Montreal's Théâtre Quat'Sous, and in 2006, he was appointed the Artistic Director of the National Arts Centre, French Theatre.

SHELLEY TEPPERMAN is a Montréal-based dramaturg and translator. She has translated more than 25 plays into English from French, Spanish and Italian, working with theatres across the country as well as the Canadian Broadcasting Corporation. She has translated four of Wajdi Mouawad's plays.

ဌ ဌ ဌ

### Synopsis

ALPHONSE, a remarkable boy with a huge imagination, has not come home and everyone is searching for him: His parents, his friends, his teachers, the police. Meanwhile, ALPHONSE is walking along a country road inventing the extraordinary adventures of Pierre-Paul Rene, "a gentle boy with a one-note voice who is never surprised by anything." Led by the NARRATOR, we jump into a multi-layered tale that bounces back and forth between the search for ALPHONSE, and the fantastic quest of Pierre-Paul Rene. In the process we experience a powerful reflection on the joy and pain of being young and what is lost in crossing the threshold to adulthood.

The full script of *Alphonse* is available from Playwrights Canada Press, www.playwrightscanada.com.

## *Alphonse*

### The Real Reason Alphonse Would Get Up In the Middle of the Night.

**NARRATOR**     Alphonse would get up each night to meet—in the hallway that led to the kitchen—Pierre-Paul-Rene, a gentle boy with a one-note voice who was never surprised by anything, and who only he, Alphonse, was acquainted with. In the time it took to go from the bedroom to the kitchen, Alphonse and Pierre-Paul-Rene could live out a thousand adventures in the dark.

Pierre-Paul-Rene always appeared to him at night since it was during a ferocious stormy night when Alphonse had gotten up to get a glass of water that they met for the first time.

On that unforgettable night Alphonse had found himself sitting up in his bed, his eyes wide open; the surrounding darkness stuck its tongue out at him.
In the next bed his brother was fast asleep and seemed totally consumed by mysterious affairs no-one else had access to.

The closed shutters painted the room a thick jelly-black. The storm was magnificent. Alphonse was very thirsty. The kitchen was far away. Very far away. Between the kitchen and Alphonse lay the hallway, and in the hallway anything could happen. Because first, Alphonse had to go all the way down the hallway to reach the switch that would fill it all with light. The hallway. That cold hallway that led to a bottomless living room and a dining room that loudly digested creaky wood. Alphonse's pyjamas were too big, too long. Getting out of bed seemed unthinkable under such conditions. But he was so thirsty and the water would be so nice and cool in the earthenware jug.

His brother rolled over. Waking him up would unquestionably jeopardize his internal affairs.

The hallway furrowed its eyebrows at him. Alphonse was terrorized! And he knew very well that he couldn't even consider waking up his mother. Because she was certain to get angry and that would be awful. "Really, Alphonse, you're not a little boy anymore," was what she said to him the last time. But now the horrible thirst ravaging his throat was so unbearable it made him forget his fear for an instant and coaxed him out of his bed. By the time he reached the edge of the hallway, it was too late to turn back! The storm kept on crashing louder and louder, and in a flash of lightning the hallway filled with sordid characters lurking at the foot of the wall... the floor was non-existent, and falling into the void seemed inevitable. And then! Right then, in a flash of lightning, Alphonse saw, at the other end of the hallway—for just a brief moment—a boy looking right at him.

"Alphonse!" He thought he heard in the middle of the storm. —"Who are you?"
—"I'm Pierre-Paul-Rene! A gentle boy with a one-note voice and I'm never surprised by anything. I've come to live inside your head, Alphonse. From now on you won't be afraid when you get up in the middle of the night and unafraid you'll cross the hallway to get your glass of water because I will always be there."

And that was it!

That night, when he went back to bed, Alphonse dreamed about Pierre-Paul-Rene... strange dreams, very strange dreams...

photo by John Lauener

Clockwise from top, Lauren Brotman, Amber Godfrey, Diana Tso, Christina Sicoli and Andrea Donaldson in *And, by the way Miss...*, 2004.

## *And, by the way Miss...* by URGE

URGE is a music driven interdisciplinary performance ensemble founded in 1991. The group has created several theatre pieces including *She promised she'd bake a pie...* and the Dora nominated *Trousseau/True Nature*. Theatre Direct Canada commissioned URGE to create a piece for grade 7 and 8 girls. The current team of Linda C. Smith, Marie Josee Chartier and Katherine Duncanson, led by founder Fides Krucker with the dramaturgical assistance of Joanna McIntyre, created *And, by the way Miss...* on an ensemble of emerging professional actors. This collaboration went on to win both performance and production Dora awards.

ᔕ ᔕ ᔕ

### Synopsis

Through workshops and discussions with young girls between the ages of 12 and 14, in schools, and in various other settings, the artists collected the stories, the thoughts and the feelings of these young girls, and promised to reflect them back to girls in a play that honoured their experience.

The URGE artists then gathered a group of young emerging female performers who they mentored through a workshop process as together they created this interdisciplinary work *And, by the way Miss...*

While the piece is heavily movement, sound and image driven, it is anchored by a series of powerful monologues revealing the inner worlds of the girls AMBER, ANDY, CHRISTINA, DIANA, and LAUREN, as they cautiously step through the minefield of early adolescence. All of the characters are dealing with the common challenges of puberty, peer relationships, changing family dynamics, and school pressures.

The full script of *And, by the way Miss...* is available from Theatre Direct.

# And, by the way Miss...

*extraordinary space*

LOCATION: *washroom #4*

TIME: *after no lunch, day 2*

**CHRISTINA** *(downstage right, clearly alone in the bathroom)* Watch it!... Watch it!... such an idiot.... It's cool... cool... *(deep breath)* Hello my name is Chrisina *(high pitch)*... Chrisitina *(deep but not sexy)* ...my name is Chrisitna *(normal)* ...Where you from? My Mom— *(sigh of disgust)*.... Where you from? Mars... *(uneasy laugh)* no no.... Where you from? my bum *(laugh)* ...just kidding... just kidding.... Barrie.... I'm just from Barrie... *(looking into the mirror)* Mirror Mirror on the wall who's the skinniest of them all?

> GIRLS, *upstage right, feel their hips with their hands, a movement chorus seen by the audience but not CHRISTINA.*

SO WHY DID YOU COME HERE? Um because my school didn't accept aliens! No... no... because I am secretly a psycho... no no kidding... because I killed a cat. No I'm totally serious. One time I was in the school washroom and this cat was just watching me from outside the window. It was watching me like I was doing something wrong—like eating one square of a chocolate bar in a washroom stall was a crime. I go running! *(She runs fast, on the spot through following chorus movements till slightly out of breath.)*

> GIRLS *bend over.*

I do sit ups.

> GIRLS *into staccato sit ups.*

> GIRLS *come up with soft bellies and explore them during this next text, some are curious, some disgusted.*

So I lured it in with a piece of chocolate. Right into my stall. And that's when it started attacking me—hissing, scratching, pouncing on me, accusing me of stuffing my face. JUST EAT IT.... No... get it away... SWALLOW IT.... No I can't.... YOU'RE SO FAT.... I knew exactly what it was doing shoving all that chocolate down my throat. Trying to kill me... and I couldn't breathe... I started to panic.... So I grabbed the cat and I strangled it *(makes the cat noise)* and I shoved it into the toilet. Get it out of me! Get out of me! *(pause)* SO WHY DID YOU REALLY COME HERE?

> *GIRLS move into Skeletor bodies, arms stretched high, walking on tip-toes, cheeks sucked in. A grotesque parody of runway models.*

…because my old friends called me Skeletor and I liked it.

## And, by the way Miss...

*extraordinary space*

*LOCATION: in the principal's office*

*TIME: afternoon into night, Day 3*

**LAUREN**   *(emerging from the clump of girls, post schoolyard fight)* Oh and by the way, Miss, that's not what happened... *they* started with *me*. I just stood there, okay. *(mosquito sound starts on a single pitch)*

But then that hot cold feeling started building up in me... I don't know. I can't explain it, okay. See, you think because I'm fourteen that I must be "out of control." Yeah well, one night I was going up to my room and I accidentally knocked over this vase that was like 150 years old or something. You want to talk out of control? Well, why don't we talk about what happened when my dad came up the stairs. *(GIRLS are moving forward with mosquito sounds—AMBER and CHRISTINA cross behind.)*

That yelling... *(ensemble—mosquito sound escalating)* it was echoing inside my head. My ears were ringing and I just wanted to punch it out of me.

"What are you? Stupid?" *(On an intake of breath, each GIRL has a short, sharp reaction as if she had been yelled at too, then silence.)*

"No, Dad, it was an accident..."

"Shut up. You are going to pay for this, little girl!" *(mosquitoes start)*

"Dad you're hurting me, please stop." *(Each GIRL, including LAUREN, does a small shoulder gesture to indicate a bit of pain, trying to get the father to take his hand away.)*

*(mosquitoes continue—GIRLS bend down)* I just dove on her. I couldn't help it. *(The ensemble slowly over the next line lifts LAUREN in a seated position. Escalating sound of mosquito.)* It was like four hundred pounds of pressure building up inside me and I kept telling myself "Walk away, walk away." *(The ensemble carries her 2 steps downstage.)* But I couldn't stop

hitting her. My fists... I swear to God. I don't know. Okay. I couldn't stop. *(mosquitoes stop abruptly)*

> *The ensemble gradually brings LAUREN to a standing position throughout the next lines.*

Everyone was staring at me. I felt ashamed and guilty and I just wanted to take it all back. I'm not a hateful person, all right? It's not who I am.

> *LAUREN's feet on ground; ensemble sets her down—like a girls' choir sings "My Favourite Things"—only the first verse—they fade back to screens—then rejoin LAUREN in the school hallway at end of next paragraph—watching.*

*(LAUREN includes some singing of pitches.)* I just feel like whenever I want to let something out I hold it in and every time I want to hold something in I let it out. It's like I have two stomachs. There's the one that I can touch with my hand, and then there's the other one... it's like it's really far down, under my skin... it's always hurting and tight and it makes me feel anxious and nervous. *(Here the GIRLS are fading out and by "Just a bit," the last one is watching.)* I just want that pit in my stomach out of me. I just want it to spread out a little bit. Just a bit. *(crossing her arms)* And that's all I have to say, Miss.

Tanya Pillay (back) and Ash Knight in *Beneath the Banyan Tree*, 2005.

*photo by Neil Kinnear and Leslie Chung*

## Beneath the Banyan Tree by Emil Sher

EMIL SHER's work includes stage plays, screenplays, radio dramas and essays. Previous plays include *Sanctuary*, a one-act play that has been staged in Canada, the U.S., Britain and Australia, *Derailed* and *Mourning Dove*, a play inspired by the Robert Latimer story. "Café Ole," his first feature film, was honoured by the Writers Guild of Canada as one of the top ten scripts of 2002. Emil's radio plays have been broadcast around the world. His most recent play, *Hana's Suitcase*, based on the book by Karen Levine, is currently touring Canada and the United States, and has been translated into Japanese.

ဢ ဢ ဢ

### Synopsis

*Beneath the Banyan Tree* explores the immigration experience of a young girl who has recently moved to Canada from India. Over the course of one day, we witness ANJALI's struggle to adjust to her new life and her efforts to "fit in." We also witness how new-found friendship, family, and the power and richness of her culture provide her with the strength to be herself.

The story takes place in three locations: ANJALI's home, her school, and in the colourful landscape of her imagination. MAITRI, the spirit of the Banyan Tree, and three engaging animal characters from the Indian Panchatantra inhabit the latter. It is in the comfort of this imagined world that ANJALI receives much needed guidance and insight.

The full script of *Beneath the Banyan Tree* is available from Theatre Direct.

## Beneath the Banyan Tree

*ANJALI soon manages to become part of the fun—hopscotch and ball games—only to see SKYLAR arrive and create friction. ANJALI stumbles and falls to her knees. As the performers move around her, focused on their schoolyard games, MASON spins away from the crowd and makes his way toward ANJALI.*

**MASON**    Are you okay?

*ANJALI looks up at MASON.*

You're bleeding.

**ANJALI**    What?!

**MASON**    On your forehead.

**ANJALI**    It's not a cut. It's a *bindi*.

*She peels the* bindi *off to show him*

**ANJALI**    See?

**MASON**    Cool!

**ANJALI**    It's not cool, Mason. It's a million miles from cool.

**MASON**    Why are you wearing it?

**ANJALI**    My grandmother just about forced me to.

**MASON**    Why?

**ANJALI**    It's my birthday.

**MASON**    Happy birthday!

**ANJALI**    *(half-hearted)* Thanks.

*MASON follows ANJALI's sightlines and sees she's eyeing SKYLAR.*

**MASON**    She's laughed at me, too. Called me names. *(beat)* Skylar laughs at everybody. *(pause)* Can I wear a *bindi*?

*MASON's request stops ANJALI in her tracks.*

**ANJALI**    No.

**MASON**     Why not?

**ANJALI**     Because.

**MASON**     Because I'm not Indian?

**ANJALI**     Because you're a boy. Boys don't wear *bindis*.

**MASON**     Says who?

**ANJALI**     That's just the way it is, Mason.

**MASON**     So that's the way it has to be?

> *ANJALI hesitates, then takes out her package of bindis from her backpack and gives one to MASON. He places it on his forehead. ANJALI laughs.*

**ANJALI**     You look silly.

**MASON**     I feel… cool. *(beat) Bindi Man!*

**ANJALI**     You better take it off.

**MASON**     Why?

**ANJALI**     I don't know. *(beat)* You're going to get laughed at.

**MASON**     So let her laugh. I don't care.

**ANJALI**     You don't?

**MASON**     *(pause)* I do. But I'll still wear it.

> *ANJALI looks at MASON in silent admiration.*

> *MASON starts to drum on his bongo. He then lifts up the drum by way of introduction.*

Harold, meet Anjali. Anjali, meet Harold.

**ANJALI**     *(smiling)* Pleased to meet you.

**MASON**     That's what other kids said when I showed them Harold. But the next thing I know, they're telling everyone I talk to a drum. That's when the names started. *(beat)* Bongo Breath. Bam Bam.

**ANJALI**     There's nothing wrong with talking to drums, or trees. *(pause)* I talk to Maitri.

**MASON**     You talk to trees?

**ANJALI**   *(defensive)* You talk to drums.

**MASON**   *(beat)* I like talking to you.

**ANJALI**   Same here.

**MASON**   When I drum, it's... I don't know. It's like I'm in my own world. No one's laughing. No one bugs me. *(beat)* It's just me and Harold.

**ANJALI**   Can I see Harold?

**MASON**   He is shy.

**ANJALI**   I know what that's like.

> *MASON drums. ANJALI begins to move to the rhythm and is soon dancing. They end on the same beat.*

**MASON**   Cool!

> *ANJALI sits back down beside MASON.*

So, are you nervous?

**ANJALI**   No, are you?

**MASON**   Nope. But it's not my turn for "All about me!"

**ANJALI**   Oh no! Is that today?

> *ANJALI is gripped with apprehension. She turns to MAITRI.*

## Beneath the Banyan Tree

**MAITRI**     Come sit by my trunk. I will tell you the story of "The Lovely Girl Who Went on a Long, Long Trip."

**ANJALI**     That's not in the Panchatantra.

**MAITRI**     Never mind. It's a good story. It begins in India.

**ANJALI**     I see...

**MAITRI**     A village where this young girl loved to play.

**ANJALI**     What was her name?

**MAITRI**     *(pause)* Maple leaf... ata.

**ANJALI**     *(Laughs)* Mapleleafata? That's not an Indian name.

**MAITRI**     They called her Lefata for short. You see, this story ends in Canada. Lefata was moving to Canada. She was excited but frightened. She was sad to leave her friends, but knew she would make new ones. There was so much about India she loved and there was much to learn about Canada. Lefata needed help finding her way in a new country where it was easy to get lost.

**ANJALI**     *(dreading the memory)* My first day at school.

**MAITRI**     Everything was different but much was the same. People are people are people.

**ANJALI**     Not all people are nice.

**MAITRI**     Not all people are nice all the time. This is true. This was one of many lessons Lefata learned listening to Panchatantra stories as she grew up. When Lefata arrived in Canada, she learned it was not easy being the new kid on the block.

**ANJALI**     A long block.

**MAITRI**     Some days she was laughed at. Some days she felt as small and timid as a mouse. Some children made fun of the clothes she wore and the food she ate.

**ANJALI**     Skylar!

**MAITRI**  But other children gave her a smile as sweet as the sweetest mango.

**ANJALI**  Mason!

**MAITRI**  Some teachers were firm but gentle.

**ANJALI**  Like a tree!

**MAITRI**  Some days Lefata was up. Some days she was down. One day, Lefata had to share a story at school.

**ANJALI**  *(desperate)* Which story?

**MAITRI**  Everyone has a story Anju. *(beat)* Every person. Every animal. Every tree has a story to tell. Yours begins in India.

**ANJALI**  I'm not in India anymore.

**MAITRI**  India is in you.

**ANJALI**  I live in Canada.

**MAITRI**  You've only been here a short time, Anju.

**ANJALI**  I have to tell my story this afternoon. *(beat)* I don't know where to start.

**MAITRI**  Not all stories have words.

**ANJALI**  How can you tell a story without words?

**MAITRI**  When a bird flies, that is a story. When a flower blooms, that is a story. When a baker bakes, or a painter paints, or a drummer drums...

**ANJALI**  Or a dancer dances!

**MAITRI &**
**ANJALI**  That is a story!

How did you get to be so smart?

*MAITRI laughs, then becomes GAMPU.*

## The Demonstration
### devised by Mark Cassidy with the company

Forging a dynamic and unpredictable piece of theatre, *The Demonstration* is a potent mix of physical, vocal, and musical energy where the intimate collides with the global, and the personal fuses with the political. *The Demonstration* is a relevant and timely theatrical happening for young people in their pre-voting years.

Described as a "kinetic meditation on democracy," director Mark Cassidy drew on material discovered through a two-year process, which involved workshops with youth and young artists as well as specially commissioned writings from playwrights Marjorie Chan, Lisa Codrington, Dave Deveau, Dawn Dumont, and Soraya Peerbaye.

## *Vegas* by Lisa Codrington

LISA CODRINGTON is an actor/writer originally from Winnipeg. She has been Playwright-in-residence at Theatre Direct and is Co-director of Youth Initiatives at Nightwood Theatre where her first play, *Cast Iron,* received its world premiere in association with Obsidian Theatre Company. It was subsequently published by Playwrights Canada Press, and was nominated for the Governor General's Literary Award for Drama in 2006. This past year Lisa performed in the Mirvish production of *'da kink in my hair,* her company Back Row Theatre, in association with Nightwood, toured *Cast Iron* to Barbados and her first radio drama, *Skylar* aired on CBC Radio.

∽   ∽   ∽

**Synopsis**

For the most part I write to try and answer questions that I have. In this piece I attempted to uncover how much people are willing to give up in order to fit in. I chose to tackle this by looking specifically at race. The days of segregation are done: Black and white are free to integrate, but can integration go too far? What happens when all one Black mother wants is for her daughter to fit in and what happens when that daughter resists?

—Lisa Codrington

The full script of *The Demonstration* is available from Theatre Direct.

## *The Demonstration* • *Vegas*

*VEGAS flips through a book of Norman Rockwell Paintings.
She chuckles, and rolls her eyes as she goes through the book
looking at the paintings. She stops when she gets to "The
Problem We All Live With." She stares at the painting for
a moment then speaks.*

**VEGAS**    Do you know Norman Rockwell's 1964 painting, "The
problem we all live with"? *(VEGAS shows, "The Problem We
All Live With.")* I used to think, if I could get this way of walking down... this pose... this posture... this strength... this
belief... this power and pride... this... this whatever you
want to call it. Thought if I could walk to school like this...
I'd be fine.

But I was a bowlegged cowboy with a malformed skull,
Bones were so soft, my eyeball fell out and rolled away,
Under the couch where the springs poked through,
Under the couch where my mom lazed away the day,
Which started the Tuesday my dad ran away.

My mom would rather be crammed up in a suburban one-
room Bachelor
Than rot in the downtown core with our brothers and sisters,
the blue-collar working poor.
It's was quite the chore, trying to keep up with all the white
collar folklore
Especially after my dad took what my mom called a detour
But what I liked to call moved in with a white woman named
Eleanor.
Guess she didn't have to work so hard for that suburban
lustor
None the less my mom still waited by the door

That is when she wasn't sleeping in the closet on the floor.
She'd rather not let anyone know what the hide-a-bed was for
Which is why she was always on me about sleeping in the
pantry more.
"Just like a two bedroom" she'd say.

Then she'd tell me to, "get my ass back to class," even though
I told her

I was a c-curve of despair,
Twisted like the hard knots she straightened out of her hair.
But my mom didn't care,
She was blinded by the glare,
And too busy wishing that her skin was a little more fair.
That's why she hid in the closet like a plump little pear
She was trying to pass, hoping not to be rare.

Still does, even to this day.

Just yesterday I tried to coax her out. Told her closets are for
other secrets and that she'd have to pick another room... not
the pantry though... cause there is barely enough space for
me and the broom... and the bathroom's out cause there's
that smell that continues to loom... oh, and the kitchen, well
that ain't even a room.
Thought I made a break through, but she just went off.

> *VEGAS lectures as her MOTHER. She does not mock her*
> *mother, rather preaches and lectures just as her MOTHER*
> *would. In other words she becomes her MOTHER.*

Vegas why must you always get so bent out of shape?
There are some for whom what was once their freezer is now
a boat if they want to stay afloat.
There are even more for whom a superdome has now become
a home.
I just want to sit in the closet for two minutes alone.
But if things are so bad, you might as well get child and
family services on the phone.

It is the new normal to redefine places of refuge so why can't
the closet be used to repress the secrets held by people of a
variety of cultures, races and sexual preferences? Especially
now in this time of terror, we should all be equally entitled to
put our secret fears in the closet if we choose.
Nature is rebelling, the earth is shaking and the sea is
swelling so we all need a safe place to hide *(pause)* inside.
THIS is homeland security my dear.

*(quietly in confidence)* ONE MUST MAKE DO with what one
has in these trying times. THAT is why everyone should all
be equally entitled to put their secret fears in the closet IF
they choose.

This is a FREE, DEMOCRATIC, MULTICULTURAL society and no one should be racially profiled out of their freedom to hide.
This is progress my dear.
The days of segregation are done.
Always remember "The Problem We All Live With."

*VEGAS looks at the painting of "The Problem We all Live With" and speaks as herself again.*

I threw my back out carrying my mom's facade which is why I never went to school.

*(Referring to "The Problem We All Live With" VEGAS tries to take Ruby's pose in the picture)* I never felt as strong as her...

Little Ruby Bridges
In a starched white dress
Walking to an all white school in New Orleans...

My mom would say, "It takes a brave little Black girl to walk with such pride and strength in a starched white dress"
But there I was, not even living in that mess
But when it came to school, I'd stress.

I used to think that if I could get this way of walking down I'd walk to school strong and proud. But all the time I spent in the pantry, got me bent outta shape.
Like I said, I was a bowlegged cowboy with a malformed skull,
So standing tall from morning till dawn,
Insisting on a new political view,
And demanding changes far overdue *(pause)* woulda been a bit much.

## *Nelly* by Dave Deveau

DAVE DEVEAU is a playwright, dramaturg, librettist, actor and videomaker. His plays include *The Fat Kid Dreams*, *Ugly Girl*, *Echoing*, *Cannibal Heat*, and *Nelly*, part of *The Demonstration* for Theatre Direct. As a librettist, he has created *Rest in Peace*, *Declining* and *Unfamiliar* for Tapestry New Opera Works. Dave translated / directed the English world premiere of Michel Tremblay's *The Train* and has spent two seasons on Nickelodeon's "Are You Afraid of the Dark?." His video "Belly" premiered in Toronto and is now circulating festivals worldwide. He is a graduate of York University and currently studies at the University of British Columbia.

သ သ သ

### Synopsis

When presented with the task of writing a piece dealing with democracy and exploring a young voice, I was immediately compelled to explore the idea of gender and identity. Identity is a core concept for everyone, but it specifically begins to creep into our thought processes as we enter our teen years. There are certain socially ascribed extremes that we are conditioned to believe. At a most basic level of these extremes is gender and how it permeates our every move and decision process. But what if your physiology is not representative of your identity? What if no physiology is? As a society, we present few options for people whose gender identity is not explicitly clear. Nelly stems from the exploration of the democracy of gender and identity—how we perceive ourselves as compared to how we're perceived, and whether there is any justice in the coming together of those two worlds.

—Dave Deveau

## *The Demonstration* • *Nelly*

*NELLY, a thirteen-year-old androgynous boy, stands in front of a mirror. A backpack sits on the floor beside it. The mirror is such that his reflection is not visible to the audience. He studies himself for a long time before beginning to speak.*

**NELLY**    They nearly butchered a boy at the mall today, you know. A whole group of them. I didn't see it exactly, I was a floor up and when I glanced over the railing, all I could see was frantic movement. And security got called. Not that that really means anything because they get called for whatever, whenever anything happens, really. But this time it seemed a bit more serious.

The cops arrived too. Yeah, the pigs, the real thing, not just the rent-a-cops, cuz it's not like they're a threat. And that's when I left. Not because I'd done anything wrong, but because I just didn't want to be involved. Or at least be perceived to be involved, you know, "perception rules over intent" according to the gospel of my father. No, I left because, you know, what if they wanted witnesses? Not that I was even a witness because all I saw was a group of people all gathered around this guy. A lot of pushing and pulling, I don't know. But I could tell that something wasn't right. You know, like a gut instinct. So maybe it's not fair to say that he was getting butchered, or even that it was a boy, but sometimes you can imagine the way things play out and just feel confident that that's the reality.

But, like I said, I don't know what it was about, so it's best that I don't say anything about it. Because then they'll want to know more and they'll have to take down my information in case they want to contact me. Like they have some notebook where they write these things down—just the basics, name, address, gender. Which seems easy enough, probably, you know, by the book, just the basics that don't really even require any thought, but then they'd get this look of panic on their face as they'd be trying to assess, you know, boy, girl, boy, girl. It would create this awkward silence between us. They'd be unsure of what to say and I'd just keep my mouth shut for the time being, right? I guess just to watch them squirm. Finally they'd give up and ask me for ID which normally I wouldn't even have on me because I don't carry it around. So then they'd get suspicious and it'd look like I'm involved somehow. And I don't want that. So I just avoided the whole thing and took off as soon as I saw the pigs.

*NELLY moves away from the mirror.*

That's how the whole thing happened.

Frankly I think I'm old enough to be able to dress myself. Ultimately it's my body and my decision, right? If my body is my temple, then I can decide how to adorn it. I don't know if my body is a temple or what, but at the very least it houses me. And therefore I can choose how I want my walls, my exterior, my shell, if you will, to be received, and perceived, and believed. It's not any different than the close attention father dearest pays to it. I can choose how I want to be perceived the same way father dearest pays to his tie selection every morning, depending on who he'll be negotiating with that day. That decision is all in the name of presentation. And I just think "what, Dad? What's so different about your clothing in a meeting compared to my clothing in life. Which one's more real?"

Who's more real?

Earlier I was staring at those boys in the food court and I could tell that they'd put a lot of thought into what they were wearing. Not necessarily effort, but they certainly have thought about what their clothing says about them. Like, "oh, my big pants and my skater shoes, I'm such a boy." Like this subversive commentary about their gender, subconscious as it may be. And yeah, actually, I do know how to use subversive in a proper context. Don't even. But with those boys in the food court, sitting there eating their A&W, that was the first thing I noticed you know? Not the food, but their existence as boys. I didn't even control it. It was completely instinctual to want to identify that. Because, you know, without a gender we don't know what to do because it toys with one of the absolutes that we believe. That some people believe. That I can't believe.

And that is what was in the back of my mind while my family gathered outside the Wal-Mart Portrait Studio. My mom, bless her heart, thinks its so great having a Wal-Mart in the mall because then we never have to leave in order to find everything we could ever need. Like this is the embodiment of innovation. So we gather outside there, my mother in some kind of summery getup and my dad with a carefully chosen tie, and his usual suit. Katie, my sister, is wearing what I remember as her prom dress and Katrina, her twin, in Katie's prom dress from last year (she would have worn her own, but during her desperate-to-be-political phase she focused all of her energy on hating the very idea of prom and never got one). Dad had picked the twins up from their school, but as I don't go to their school, lucky me, I told them I'd just take the bus and meet them at the mall. The bus isn't glamorous, I know, but there's less bickering that way. Unless the driver wants to give me hell. And he doesn't. Believe me.

So I end up changing in the family washroom because there's privacy there and it saves the whole "which door's safer" routine that I'm always going through at school, and I take the time to really, you know, get ready with Daddy-o's haunting "if we're going to do the photo, we're going to do it right" at the back of my mind, thinking "Dad, why do you speak in colloquial catchphrases?" Wishing he'd at least pick up on my use of alliteration.

So I meet them, freshly schooled, freshly changed in the bowels of the mall bathroom and as soon as they see me I hardly even have reaction time. I can just see it in their eyes immediately, this twinge of disbelief that they don't know if they should let out or repress. It stifles the "Hi" I'm attempting to get out and I end up just standing there.

Dad looks at Mom as Katie and Katrina share one of their looks that they always share whenever they don't approve of something, which is all the time. And everyone's silent, just for a moment. And it's so clear what all of this is about. Because Dad had actually sat me down the previous night in order to make sure that I wouldn't cause a "scene."

*As NELLY's FATHER.*

**FATHER**     Go with your gut, but in doing so, respect your elders. That's me and your mother. And your grandparents.

But they're not here, so that's a moot point. So think before you speak. Is that clear?

*As NELLY.*

**NELLY**    Yeah, sure, Dad, practically layman's terms. It would seem he'd just wanted to clarify the dress code for us to get our family portrait done and how I'd have to think carefully about what I wanted to look like in the photo, like I said the usual tirade about 'perception etc etc etc' and that we would be sending them to both sets of grandparents and to my various aunts, all of whom are old maids. Who's more real there? And he was really firm in leading me to believe that it was ultimately my choice, but that I should think about it…. And I did. A lot. And it led me to certain decisions.

And thus I showed up… dressed to the nines. In a dress. A real dress.

> *NELLY takes a dress from his backpack and stands in front of the mirror, holding it up and admiring his reflection.*

It even had a crinoline. Maybe that's what the big deal was, maybe it was that I looked far better than Katie or Katrina could ever hope to, because certainly everyone had already seen their grad dresses, even the grandparents because they're always asking for pictures of the twins. But at that moment Mom finally parts her lips and out it comes. It's beyond expected at this point and I just want to know how explosive it's going to be. I'm edgy with my anticipation. And her lips part further and sound comes out and I notice Katie and Katrina reacting but I'm not really hearing it; I'm sort of frozen mid thought, on the brink of reacting and then it lands.

*As NELLY's MOM.*

**MOM**    NELSON!

*As NELLY.*

**NELLY**    There's a finger waving in my face and it's already getting attention from other patrons wandering around the mall, they're gawking as they divert their children's eyes, thinking they don't want them to grow up to be like me and so if they don't see me then maybe I don't exist. But they're so wrong—because even if it's just the very idea of me, I do exist and I want to challenge their children to look at me.

*As NELLY's MOM.*

**MOM**   Nelson.

*As NELLY.*

**NELLY**   She says, in that firm, "I'm taking control as the family matriarch and you will obey everything I say" tone.

*As NELLY's MOM.*

**MOM**   Nelson, you will take off that dress and put on something appropriate.

*As NELLY.*

**NELLY**   I don't want to respond because she knows that I never answer people who address me with my full name, and so until I hear the words Nelly come out of her mouth she may as well just stop. "That's not my name, mother!" And then it's the eye-roll and I know that the war's just begun. The mothers are milling about and I can hear wisps of conversation from the expecting mothers, and the grandmothers talking about growing up in their day and how that never would have happened.

*As NELLY's MOM.*

**MOM**   Nelson, how dare you...

*As NELLY.*

**NELLY**   And those are the magic words that just make me shut right off.

Mom's still talking and I'm making it clear that the conversation's over, half of me wanting to head back to the family washroom just to admire the dress in the privacy of the dirty mirror under bad neon light, but at least somewhere. Somewhere that isn't here in this moment. I even consider sprinting through the mall, making everyone gasp at the sight of me, showing off to the A&W boys.

And then it happens. Mom's right in front of me, really close and she begins grabbing at the dress, seemingly trying to tear it off as if my nudity wouldn't be more of a scandal. Then my father's moving and I think he's coming to my help, to calm her down, drag her off to the McDonald's beside the portrait studio just to ease her mind or something, buy her the two sundaes for two dollars that she loves so much, but he doesn't. He joins her. The look in his eye echoing the look from our meeting last night. Then Katie and Katrina aren't far behind.

There's other people, the gawking mothers who have joined in, no longer hiding their children's faces, but encouraging them to join in and they're trying to tear off the ribbon around me, and then the outer layers, the sleeves, starting at the seams and continuing deeper and deeper, past the crinoline. And it doesn't stop. They're trying to tear me apart, limb from limb. More and more of them join in, a sea of them. I'm being swarmed. I'm completely surrounded and I don't know what to say or do. And I can feel my joints and ligaments starting to separate. Hear the severing of my body. And I could swear that I'm floating out of it. I can see in my peripheral vision that mall security has shown up, and the police are arriving too, they're not far behind. The real ones, the pigs, not the rent-a-cops.

In the midst of all of this I stare up, looking in a final desperate attempt, for a way out of this, of all of this. And I see it. Standing there observing with this touch of concern, this look of not really being able to discern what's happening, but feeling some sort of compassion for the victim there, unsure of where to look, where to focus... it's... it's me. And I stare into my own eyes, pleading for support. And once again it's like time is standing still. I await some sort of response and then it seems like it's coming. And I start to see myself move my feet, a step forward, and then leaning on the railing, trying to get a good look, but not really being sure of what's being seen, and this look of concern coming over my face, I see my eyes shift to the cops and back to me, and then... then... I'm running away so as to not have witnessed it. And everyone is all around me, and I catch my father's eyes. And who's more real now, Dad? Who's more real? And then I'm gone. I'm gone in all regards.

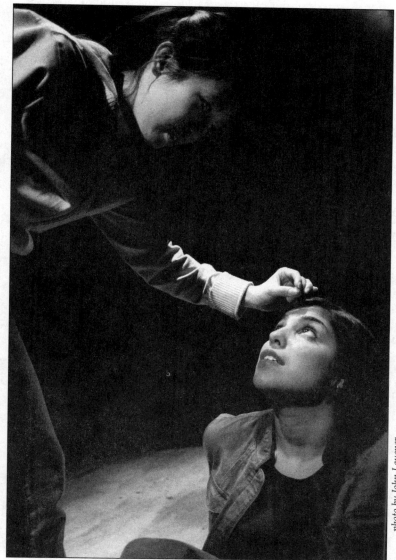

*photo by John Lauener*

Ella Chan (standing) and Nisha Ahuja in *The Demonstration*, 2006.

## *The Madness of the Square* by Marjorie Chan

Marjorie Chan is an award-winning playwright and performer based in Toronto. She is passionate about creating art with and for youth. As a writer she has been invited to the writers' units at Nightwood Theatre, Factory Theatre, Tapestry New Opera Works and the Banff Centre for the Arts. She has also been Playwright-in-Residence for Theatre Direct Canada and Cahoots Theatre Projects. Her other works for young people include the opera *Sanctuary Song* (with composer Abigail Richardson) and the puppet play *Sweet Protest*.

∽  ∽  ∽

### Synopsis

In 1989 I was fifteen. At fifteen I was brave and bold. I wanted to save the world. In spring, I wrote letters. In summer, I marched in protest. In autumn, I held fundraisers. And in the winter, I carried anti-fur flyers in my knapsack and would sidle up to unsuspecting fur coats and slip them in the pocket. I was even... vegetarian. Not as much of a shock to my Chinese parents as I desired, because they could at least relate my latest aberration to Buddhism. I wore gypsy earrings and fringe and Birkenstocks. I was young, I was idealistic. Like my protagonist I would stare up at the moon and stars and dream of a future.

Then, then the massacre of Tiananmen in June 1989 played out on my big-screen TV in the suburbs. I grew up. It was harder to dream. It was harder to be brave. It was harder to save the world.

—Marjorie Chan

## *The Demonstration • The Madness of the Square*

*FAN YING, a 20-year-old student who becomes an important student leader in Tiananmen during the 1989 protest. She is currently in hiding due to the crackdown in the aftermath of the tragedy.*

*A non-descript room with a dirt floor. The shadows of moonlight through bars.*

**FAN-YING**    My hair touches wall, my toes only have dirt, trapped
A square of my own making, my voice the creator
My beliefs the design
By me, my actions I am alone
The rules of architecture, Tiananmen
Of crisscrossing lines and stretches of stone
Deliberate, meant to be lonely bleak
An expanse without voice or heart

I never imagined famous,
As all the students became famous,
Words like gasoline leaking from an overturned bus
Words that fall out one by one like veins fed from
a still-beating heart
Words surrounded me, leading further and further away from
centre and truth
Nod, they nod nod with understanding with yeses and
thoughtful looks
The cameras roll pictures images sent far far away from this
our desolate square...
And left is my mirror me in tapes and photos
Upfront, exposed and seen,
Signed my own warrant
Not the real me... a fake a façade a make believe did I create?
Did I make this fantasy of democracy?

The moon pierces my square of sanctuary
Aglow in the night and its' midnight finger points me out and
says "She is here! Here is how to find her!"
As I wait in begged-for shadows, pierce not here, find me not
here, do not give me light, because I don't deserve it...

My enemy the moon, that casts my silhouette 'gainst
buildings in a cinematic flash as I ran as I ran
A cool reflection watching all
How else to see the pavement ripped up by tanks
How to avoid the pools of blood
How to not trip over splayed legs and open hearts
How not to see the blind worms from a soldier's intestines
ripped apart by a thriving crowd
Torn apart ripping flying flesh and bone and metal in the air
Tearing up soul and heart the idea the world
A dazzling troop of thoughts march through the night and
keep me up
Weight bearing down from my cluttered mind,
Scattered shoes and food and slit thoughts and bullets and
tents and Mao and my friends... oh my friends, my dear poor
beautiful maddening friends

Rumble rumble
My stomach or helicopters, rumble rumble...
Tanks.

They are coming.

A penetrating reality of bullets that down you, my friends
A sobering run, a coward...

Who ran.... Who ran and ran because she was lost
Who turned her back
Who stood with the students in life,
Who turned her back on the Goddess of Democracy and did
not see it fall
Who could rally when safe
But now could only scream

The madness of the square, its lines and rules straight and to
the point
When the hail of fire, the whistling of metal began I ran
And my lucky back never felt the sting
And my lucky head never felt the blow
And lucky me, to be alive to be waiting
Because they will come again
Plenty of pictures
My face, my voice in tape after tape

They will invade my small square of security
And they will take me
Until I am no more.

## About Theatre Direct

**Our Mandate:**

To commission, develop and produce Canadian plays for young people (children and youth) that provoke, challenge, question and empower our audience. To explore important issues relevant to young people using sophisticated and uncompromising theatre. To nurture our audience's appreciation of the art form, subject matter and themes through innovative and engaging arts education programs.

**Artistic Mission Statement:**

• We believe young people have the right to access and enjoy meaningful cultural experiences made especially for them therefore we strive to meet the highest artistic standards in dramaturgy, production and performance.

• We do not view children as a future audience or a monolithic market. This audience is a true reflection of the diversity of Canadian society; therefore we strive with our programming to reflect this diversity in the stories we tell and the artists that interpret them.

• We try to interpret the world through a young person's eyes and maintain awareness of global and local issues and trends in education and social policy to inform our approach.

• We are committed to ensuring access for all young people regardless of economic, physical or geographic need. This commitment informs our artistic and organizational policies and programs.

**Philosophy:**

Because we have immense faith in a young person's imaginative capacity, we strive with our productions to push theatrical boundaries. Because the world around us is diverse we strive to reflect the cultural diversity of our communities, both in the stories we tell and the people who tell them. Because we have faith in a young person's ability to contemplate difficult subject matter or issues, we never shy away from uncomfortable material, and strive to speak directly to our audience in a way that avoids preaching or lecturing.

## History:

Since its inception in 1976, Theatre Direct Canada has presented 85 productions that have reached an audience in excess of 2 million students across the country and has received numerous nominations and awards including Dora Mavor Moore Awards and Chalmers Canadian Playwrighting Awards.

Founded by respected writer, director and performer, David Craig, Theatre Direct Canada spent its first decade touring work for children to schools with engaging productions such as *Morgan's Journey* and *All for Beaver Hats*. In the 1980s, Artistic Director Susan Serran introduced plays exploring challenging issues for teens such as *Getting Wrecked* (alcohol abuse) and *Thin Ice* (date rape). The company also expressed its interest and affinity with Quebec-based theatre for young people and the introduction of different stylistic languages into the theatre presentation such as dance, multi-media and music.

Throughout the leadership of Andrey Tarasiuk from 1990 to 2001, Theatre Direct introduced Toronto to plays that are now hallmarks of excellent theatre for children such as *Andrew's Tree*, *I Met a Bully on the Hill* and *Toronto at Dreamers Rock*. The company also emphasized venue-based productions for high school youth over school touring. Free of restrictions in content and form common in a high school environment, they pushed their dramaturgical and production standards to an even greater height with groundbreaking productions such as *Flesh and Blood* (AIDS), *Little Sister* (Eating Disorders) and *A Secret Life* (Youth at Risk). In 2000, a new wave of young playwrights were premiered in two Buncha Young Artists... Festivals and continued to push artistic and thematic boundaries, speaking directly to a young adult audience.

Since 2001, Theatre Direct under the direction of Lynda Hill has taken its commitment to speaking directly to its audiences even further with works aimed specifically at narrower age groups (*Petra, And, by the way Miss...* for grades 7/8, *The Demonstration*, for grades 9/10) and works that altered the TYA landscape by reflecting and speaking from a different cultural persepctive (*The Phoenix Rides a Skateboard, Beneath the Banyan Tree*). Since 2002, the company has extended and enhanced the time spent with young people and educators around its productions through daylong programs, residencies, and comprehensive written resources.

In 2008, Theatre Direct will move to its first permanent home at the Green/Arts Barns in the West of Toronto. Its 2000 sq/ft studio space will enable the company to offer a variety of arts education activities and events as well as showcase our touring productions and the work of guest companies serving children and youth.

## Author Index

## Title Index